Evolution of Chomsky's Transformational Grammar

El Mouatamid Ben Rochd

Evolution of Chomsky's Transformational Grammar

BOD

© 2020, El Mouatamid Ben Rochd

Édition : BoD – Books on Demand

12/14 rond-point des Champs-Élysées, 75008 Paris

Impression : BoD - Books on Demand, Norderstedt, Allemagne

ISBN 9 782322203796

CONTENTS

Acknowledgment

Many thanks are due to my students, relatives, friends and colleagues in particular Dr. Khalid Chaouch, Dr. Ahmed Elheggach, Dr. Amr Sellam, Dr. Mostafa Shoul, Dr. Reitha Ben Rochd, for their invaluable help. Above all our thanks must go to Professor Avram Noam Chomsky, from whom we learnt this most elegant theory of language, which filled an infinity of hours of teaching – it is indeed GENERATIVE & TRANSFORMATIONAL.

"Money takes you nowhere,

Friends take places, indeed!"

Introduction

The material dealt with in linguistics is so vast and complicated. Languages[1] are said to be inflectional, concatenative... They belong to families: Indo-European, Semitic.., sub-families: Romance, Germanic..etc. There are old and modern, spoken and written, standard and colloquial versions of every language. In syntax - let alone the levels of linguistics - many problems exist.

The linguistic investigation of sentence structure is, in a way, similar to what happens in arithmetic theory. When a set is discovered to be inadequate to cope with a mathematical item or mathematical class, the mathematicians opt for a new set (that includes the preceding one). The subtraction 2-3 is an impossible operation within the framework of N^2 so Z is established to cope with it, but within the latter 50/3 is impossible so Q is created. $\sqrt{2}$ does not exist in Q so R is set forth. $\sqrt{-2}$ is not allowed in R so C is created and so on and so forth.

---

[1] The amazing organization of the bee colony is obviously based on their no less amazing "language". The latter system that challenged the researchers for a long time, until German Karl Von Frisch of Munich University found the solution to that mystery after spending thirty years of patient (read painful!) research and observation. (Benveniste 1966)

[2] N, R .. stand for Natural Numbers, Real Numbers, etc..

In linguistics, there are many old and new schools. Traditional grammar, the Neo-grammarians, the Tagmemic school (the followers of which believe that linguistic structure can be exhaustively accounted for in terms of SLOTS and FILLERS) and the systemic linguists who work by RANK, SYSTEM and DELICACY.

For Bloomfieldians (Bloomfield et al.) the sentence is the syntactic unit because it shows greater freedom of occurrence in speech. Every sentence is marked by a particular intonation. In writing, it starts with a capital letter and ends with a full stop, a question or an exclamation mark. They deal with the surface structure as a sequence of adjacent items, but do recognize hierarchies of immediate constituents by opposition to Ferdinand de Saussure[3] who is a 'dualist'. He distinguishes LANGUE (i.e., language) from PAROLE (i.e., speech).

Chomsky is a still more explicit 'dualist' than Saussure .He distinguishes between COMPETENCE[4] and PERFORMANCE as well as between DEEP and SURFACE STRUCTURE. His approach - a computer-like grammar (the word GENERATIVISM[5] itself is

---

[3] Last century's Philology and Evolutionist Historicism were brought to a halt when they were faced by the stumbling block of Saussurean Synchronic Structuralism.

[4] Thanks to our Linguistic Competence we know that certain pairs of words rhyme, that some phrases mean the opposite of other phrases, that some sentences are ungrammatical.

[5] Daring Chomskian rationalism, mentalism, and generativism superseded hard-line Bloomfieldian empiricism, behaviorism and

taken from mathematics) - gives us syntactic models that can predict and recognize, more or less explicitly, the sentences of natural languages.

Some psychologists assume, against Chomsky's point of view, that the deep structure matches what actually exists within the speaker's mind. Furthermore, Chomskian linguists consider the actual utterances as incomplete and non-representative, because they are continually broken by slips of tongue, self-corrections and interruptions. So the actual performance is to be replaced, in the linguistic inquiry, by the competence of an imagined ideal native speaker in an ideal speech environment (cf. Labov's Functional Competence). This process is known as "scientific idealization".

Linguistics is meant to be scientific. For the linguist's attitude is just like that of a physicist, who wants to describe, for instance, the motion of a shell. He first limits himself to four variables - say the length of the cannon, the weight of the shell, the distance of the target at and the angle made by the cannon and earth. Then, if there's and outside interference at the time of the firing like - say wind - he/she, or the engineer, will have to assess the force and the direction of the interference and correct the first equation accordingly.

Likewise in linguistics, we must limit our scope to a small area of language at the beginning. Our method

---

descriptivism respectively. This revolution started in the United States and the rest of the world followed.

must be as systematic and economic as possible. As for any empirical attempt, we must proceed from a hypothesis towards a conclusion by means of observation and testing. Ultimately, we can build a model of what natural language patterns might be. We must confine our analysis to language structure, not refer to the outside world, and express the results of our discoveries in purely formal terms.

The segmentation of language remains, however, only a matter of trial and error, far more than what happens in Physics. An unknown language can only be identified phonetically and transcribed in an impressionistic fashion. But neither phonetics nor phonology can catch other patterns bigger than the sound system. So the linguist must learn the language he wants to investigate (or, at least, use the services of informants), notice the regular occurrences of items bigger than the sound segment and ask native speakers about the relevance of the samples he may come to describe.

The linguist can also start with his own language (idiolect) and proceed gradually to the investigation of his language family, then to human language (i.e. UNIVERSAL GRAMMAR). He can also proceed from level one of linguistics to the other levels in the same language. He can use the most practical grammar (simple and accurate) available to him, try it and eventually replace it, when he comes to its limitations and discovers a better one.

After (or apart from) Phonology and Morphology, Syntax is proposed to cope with the structure of a given language. It is claimed that syntax is the key the process of learning[6] and understanding a language. The sentence is generally considered the upper unit, but syntax deals also with the clause, the phrase and the word. Syntax deals with word-relations and the structure of the sentence in the most systematic way possible.

Years ago, as I was writing at the railway station of York city, I met an English student of history. He tried to tell me about his sister who had gone sightseeing to "Tangiers in Tunisia" (sic !). Then he said that he would be delighted to come and see my country. I told him that he was "most welcome to my home in Tokyo!) We laughed a lot and he concluded saying; "Actually, you're right, I might go to a travel agency, book for a country and end up in another!"

This student of history had a good approximation (knowledge) about the geography of Africa. At least, he knew that Tangiers is a city (and not "something to eat"!). He had a second approximation which told him that it is a city in Africa and not in Asia or Australia. He

---

[6] "The fact about languages... we don't really learn anymore than we learn to have arms. It just grows. You can't help it. You speak to your child in an environment where language is being used and that child has no more choice whether to weight five pounds or something or decide not to eat. It can't decide not to learn that language. Because learning language is just a process that the brain goes through under certain conditions. It is a process of growth not a process... what people call learning. The system grows in certain ways because of the way it is built." (Chomsky 1972)

even knew that it is situated in North Africa (which is a third approximation). Of course, he needed two more approximations: he needed to shift Tangiers to the Moroccan territory and finally, spot it in the north of Morocco (fifth approximation).

Although this student may have seemed silly at first, in fact his approach is perfectly valid. It is actually used by all researchers and working scientists who are "silly", in that sense. They work by successive approximations. Likewise, the linguist works step-by-step towards a system of rules and principles that are part of the native speaker's competence. He formulates a RULE, comes across a counter-example, formulates a new rule and so on and so forth.

In syntax, this approach is applicable. Consider the rule known as QUESTION TAG:

It has a bell, hasn't it?

1st approximation:

a) locate the verb and copy it to the right of the sentence. If the original verb is positive, make the copy negative, and vice versa.

b) locate the subject of the sentence and copy it to the right of the verb.

* The boys are in town, aren't the boys?

2nd approximation:

a) locate the verb and copy it to the right of the sentence

b) if the original verb is positive, make it negative and vice versa

c) insert to the right of the verb the pronoun that agrees with the subject in person, number and gender

* John could have arrived, arrivedn't he?

* John could have arrived, hasn't he?

3rd approximation

a) copy the first verb to the right of the sentence, making the copy negative if the original verb is positive and vice versa.

b) insert to the right of the copied verb the pronoun that corresponds to the subject in person, number and gender. (Akmajian & Heny 1975)

John could have arrived, couldn't he?

In Semantics, the same scenario applies. Consider the BINDING of reflexives:

John1 saw John1 ==> John1 saw himself1

*Mary1 never talks to us about themselves1

Mary1 never talks to us about yourself1

Mary1 never talks to us about himself1

Mary1 never talks to us about herself1

1st approximation:

a reflexive is bound to any expression having the same number, gender, and person (AGREEMENT).

- What do your friends think about Fred?

- John doesn't like himself very much,

2nd approximation:

a reflexive is bound to a noun phrase in the same sentence

[s John never talks to himself about Fred]

3rd approximation:

a reflexive is bound to a noun phrase in the same clause

John thinks [c that Fred hates himself]

4th approximation:

A reflexive is bound to a noun phrase in the same clause that preceeds it. We say that they are CO-REFERENTIAL. (Radford 1981)

This book aims at presenting the successive approximations[7] that TRANSFORMATIONAL

---

[7] "(there is) a very striking difference between the natural sciences and the humanities. In the natural sciences, it is taken for granted that theories are constantly changing. We do not understand enough, even in the most intensively studied areas, to be at all confident that we know "the truth". In fact, it is taken for granted that we do not. Therefore, if theories are not changing, the field is probably dead or

GRAMMAR has gone through since its early insemination in 1957 up to the "Minimalist program3 of the late nineties. After which, there is a critical chapter I call "Occam's Razor". Finally there is a chapter on "Logical Form". (For "Phonetics Form" see Ben Rochd 1994). The appendix deals with the major early transformations of the '60s.

---

not worth pursuing because it is too trivial and boring." (Chomsky 1995)

1. CHOMSKY'S T.G.

1.1. First Version

1.1.1. Phrase Structure Rules

The Bloomfieldian linguists dealt somehow with syntax; their approach was known as the Immediate Constituent Analysis (or IC analysis for short). For instance, in an "Indian" utterance like *the boyhittheball* we would recognize only the upper unit (which is the sentence) and the lower unit (which is the sound), but in between we would be left with a problem, if not many. Fortunately, the scholars of English (as it happens to be English) have left spaces between the words. So we have the sequence: *the boy hit the ball*. To move further, we can use SUBSTITUTION, as in the sentence *John hit Mary*. To prove that *the boy* (and *a ball*) form one unit. Substitution again shows that *hit a ball* is also a unit (cf. John *came*). Finally, the upper unit as we know, is the whole sentence *the boy hit a ball*. This can be represented diagrammatically as follows:

(1)

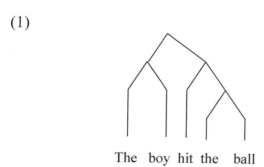

The boy hit the   ball

25

We can say that although IC analysis is very explicit, it is rather limited as it does not draw any GENERALIZATION about language. (Soams & Perlmutter, 1979) Suppose now we started from top to bottom instead of bottom upwards. We would obtain what follows:

(2)

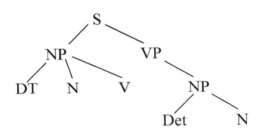

Which will generate the boy hit a ball and

the boy hit the ball and

a boy hit a ball and

a boy hit the ball and

a boy hit a boy etc.

So we can see the merits of this new approach known as PHRASE STRUCTURE GRAMMAR (or the mathematical way of dealing with sentences which is much richer).

Now a piece of terminology seems necessary:

(3)

a. ( ): the item inside the parentheses is optional, as in: the (*old*) man - *old* is optional. This is in terms of acceptability.

b. [ ]: the items included in the square brackets form a unit like [*the old man*] which is a noun phrase.

c. { }: the items included in the braces form a paradigm or table of substitution as in:

$$\left\{ \begin{array}{c} \text{he} \\ \text{the boy} \\ \text{John} \end{array} \right\}$$

d. ⟶ stands for a phrase structure rule.

e. ===> stands for a transformation.

What we have established so far is the internal structure of the sentence *the boy hit a ball*, or indeed the generative system for all the simple, declarative affirmative (KERNEL) sentences of English (at least). It is called a TREE diagram, or PHRASE MARKER (P-MARKER for short). It actually has two alternatives, the LABELLED BRACKETING as in (4):

(4) [s[NP[Det the][N boy]]]

[VP[V hit][NP[Det a][N ball]]]]]

and PHRASE STRUCTURE RULES[1]:

(5)   S ⟶ NP - VP

27

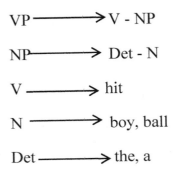

VP ⟶ V - NP

NP ⟶ Det - N

V ⟶ hit

N ⟶ boy, ball

Det ⟶ the, a

1.1.2. Transformations

Now phrase structure grammar (PS grammar for short) itself is limited. It cannot possibly generate/link all the sentences of English. It especially faces problems such as DISCONTINUITY as in the sentence: *In God, we trust.* (in the Dollar). We know intuitively that in fact it is: *we trust in God* and likewise in the sentence: *what are you looking at that woman like that for, boy?* (Griffiths, <u>Black Like Me</u>) we know intuitively that *what... for* form one unit which is *why*.

PS grammar also faces the problems of DIFFERENCE between sentences (known as PARAPHRASE) as in the following paradigm:

(6)

a. The Moors defeated the Spaniards

b. The Spaniards were defeated by the Moors

c. It was the Moors who defeated the Spaniards

d. The Moors' defeat of the Spaniards

(was total)

e. I expected the Moors to defeat the Spaniards

f. They defeated them.

Another problem faced by PS grammar (a semantic one this time) is AMBIGUITY[2]. The noun phrase *old men and women* has two meanings either *old men and old women* (the second occurrence of the adjective *old* having been deleted) or *old men and any women.*

Finally, PS grammar faces the problem of SIMILARITY. Some sentences like *John is easy to please* and *John is eager to please* seem to have exactly the same surface structure namely NP, V, Adj and S. But we know intuitively that the first sentence means something toughly like [*it is easy - someone pleases John*], whereas the second one means [*John is eager - John pleases someone*].

All these problems are solved by another grammatical rule called TRANSFORMATION. There were indeed many transformations in the early TG literature.

To take but one transformation, PASSIVE for instance, we need two main stages known as STRUCTURAL DESCRIPTION and STRUCTURAL CHANGE, as follows:

(7)

The   boy   hit   a   ball

NP$_1$	V act.	NP$_2$	: **S-D**

and

A	ball	was hit	by	the	boy

N	V pas.	by NP$_1$	: **S-C**

Three conclusions can be drawn about the first version of T.G.:

1. PS rules generate KERNEL sentences which are by definition simple, declarative and affirmative.

2. Transformations, unlike PS rules, are CONTEXT-SENSITIVE. They work according to the logical formula IF ... THEN. For instance, you cannot have passive S-C unless you have its S-D.

3. Finally, transformations are by definition MEANING PRESERING[3]. They affect the form but not the meaning of sentences. (Chomsky 1957)

Notes

1. Furthermore, those categories happen to have RECURSIVE properties. That is NPs can include other NPs within them. For instance the NP *he man who ran the Marathon* contains within it the NP *the Marathon*. So we have an infinite class of structures because of this recursive property.

30

2. *The chicken are ready to eat* has got two deep structures; either *the chicken are ready to be eaten by someone,* or *the chicken are ready to eat the grains*, say.

3. This is open to debate, consider *not many arrows hit the target / the target was not hit by many arrows.*

1.2. Standard Theory

1.2.1. Phrase Structure Rules & Lexicon

Let us now see to what extent the PS rules suggested by Chomsky in his first book <u>Syntactic Structures</u> (1957) can handle the following sentence:

(1) *sincerity may frighten the boy*

(2)   a. S $\longrightarrow$ NP - VP

     b. VP $\longrightarrow$ V - NP

     c. NP $\longrightarrow$ Det - N

     d. V $\longrightarrow$ frighten

     e. N $\longrightarrow$ sincerity

     f. Det $\longrightarrow$ the

(3)

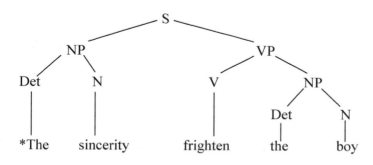

We notice above that the application of the above PS rules have left some problems and residues. For instance, the problem of tense is pending a solution and cannot be solved until we insert an Aux node as follows:

(4)   S → NP - Aux - VP

Another problem concerns the idiosyncrasy of the English sequence [Det + N] in which [+abstract] Nouns do not take the definite article. The above P-Marker will also generate * the *sincerity frighten boy* or * *the boy frightened sincerity*. Notice that the PS rules above have not respected the "personality" of the verb *frighten* in many ways. The solution suggested by the STANDARD THEORY is to draw a categorial distinction between the first three PS rules suggested by the first version (enriched with Aux) and the last three.

The difference is that the first three rules expand ABSTRACT SYMBOLS into abstract symbols; whereas the second set of rules expands symbols into actual WORDS of the language: **S → NP-Aux-VP** vs. **V → frighten**. The last three rules have been extensively developed in the Standard Theory and became the LEXICON. The latter first of all tells you that *boy* and *sincerity* are NOUNS (as a CATEGORY). This is largely similar to the traditional parts of speech but does not stop at that. It accounts also for their morphology. It divides the words (called FORMATIVES) into LEXICAL formatives like *table, follow, cat, above, etc.,* and GRAMMATICAL formatives like -s, -ed. Second, the lexicon gives you information about the SUBCATEGORIZATION of the formatives. SO verbs like *come, see, give, have (I have* *my car repaired every six months)* are INTRANSITIVE, TRANSITIVE, DITRANSITIVE and CAUSATIVE respectively (and can also mean eat). Thirdly, the lexicon includes semantic information known as SELECTIONAL RESTRICTIONS (a controversial point). Consider the following paradigm:

(5)

a. *He frightened

b. *He frightened sincerity

c. * He frightened the table

d. He frightened the boy

The first sentence is ungrammatical, because it does not respect the subcategorization of the verb frighten (a transitive verb). The second does respect its subcategorization but in the wrong way by giving it an abstract object. The third does indeed give it an [- abstract] object but [- animate]. The last sentence gives it the right object which is [+ animate] ([+ human] being redundant).

1.2.2. Transformations

After the PS RULES and THE LEXICON, the Standard Theory suggests a second type of rules; namely TRANSFORMATIONS.

(6)

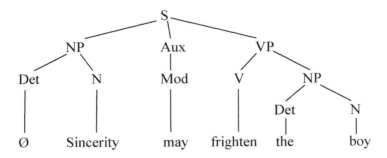

Consider again the sentence *sincerity frightened the boy*. If we apply the PS rules suggested in (4) we will obtain.

(7)

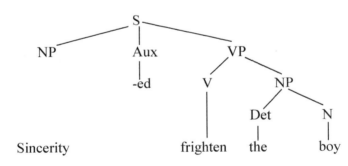

We are left with the grammatical formative *-ed* (past tense marker) on the left of the verb; a representation which is undesirable (this hypothesis has strong empirical support though, from emphasis *I did work hard*! and question *did you_work hard?*).

Chomsky suggests the application of an OBLIGATORY transformation called AFFIX HOPPING to (7) to yield (8):

(8) sincerity frighten-ed the boy.

Suppose now we had a verb like *took*, this model suggests that we would start with an abstract string called occasionally DEEP STRUCTURE) like *he -ed take the book*, but even after affix hopping has applied, we will be left with a problem of morphology: take *-ed*. To solve it we would need another obligatory transformation called MORPHOPHONEMICS:

(9) take+ed ----> took

Consider now the difference between morphophonemics and passive:

(10)

a. The boy hit+ed the ball ===> The boy hit the ball

and

b. The boy hit the ball ===> the ball was hit (by the boy)

As far as acceptability is concerned, the second sentence namely *the boy hit the ball* does not need any transformation and hence PASSIVE is an OPTIONAL transformation; whereas AFFIX HOPPING (morphophonemics in general) is OBLIGATORY (for acceptability considerations).

Finally some sentences need a transformational CYCLE. Consider the utterance *serve_yourself, won't you?* Let us try and suggest the following deep structure for it and all the way from that to the surface structure:

(11) you will serve you

A series of transformations is needed to reach the surface structure: QUESTION-TAG, IMPERATIVE DELETION and REFLEXIVIZATION. What does each one of these three transformations say? TAG: "copy Aux then make it negative and copy the subject to its right". IMPERATIVE:"delete the subject and Aux". REFLEXIVIZATION: "turn the second NP into a reflexive pronoun in case of COREFERENCE".

Let us apply these transformations as suggested.

(12) a. TAG: you will serve you ==> you will serve you, won't you?

b. IMP: you will serve you, won't you ==> serve you, won't you?

ahaa! we had no first NP to apply our reflexivization to. We have commited a BLEEDING destruction/absence of SD) to borrow Kayne's terminology. We probably need to leave imperative until the end. We have to respect a certain order called CYCLE: 1. tag, 2. reflexive, 3. imperative, or TRAFFIC RULES as Chomsky* (1965) calls them. (You don't put the shoes before the socks, do you?)

Conclusions:

a. The STANDARD THEORY suggests an ABSTRACT initial form called DEEP STRUCTURE.

b. It draws a distinction between OBLIGATORY and OPTIONAL transformations.

c. When more than one transformation is needed, we must respect a certain order called CYCLE

Notes

"Consider the sentence *John seems to be liked by Mary* which, in theory, would itself derive from a deep structure *it seems Mary likes John*, then we would have two transformations: first Passive would move *John* to the initial position of the embedded sentence *it seems John is liked by Mary*. Then a rule of Raising would raise the subject John to the initial position of the matrix sentence, yielding *John seems to be liked by Mary*". (Chomsky 1972)

1.3. Extended Standard Theory (E.S.T.)

The E.S.T. consists of: X-BAR SYNTAX, THE LEXICON, MOVEMENTS (including TRACE THEORY[1]) and CONSTRAINTS. It has probably started with Ross's *Constraints on Variables in Syntax* (MIT, Ph.D, 1968) which is second only to the "Bible" *Aspects of the Theory of Syntax* (to use Newmeyer's words).The E.S.T. is also based on Chomsky's "Remarks on Nominalization," in *Semantic Studies in Generative Grammar* (1972) and "On Wh-Movement," in *Formal Syntax* (1977).

1.3.1. X-bar theory[2]

1.3.1.1. Syntactic structures

To deal with X-BAR SYNTAX one has to consider first P.S. Grammar, and to do so one has to raise a crutial question: what is meant by a SYNTACTIC STRUCTURE? A question which is logically linked to another - namely how are we to represent it?

Suppose we started with the utterance: *kinyahakunamatata*, in some exotic language. All we could tell at first is the upper unit, i.e., the sentence and the lower unit which is the sound. So our representation would be something like:

(1) k i n y a h a k u n a m a t a t a

But obviously this is not the ideal representation of it. Fortunately, we know at least the first word of Swahili which is the name of the African country: *Kenya*[3].

Now, if we shift to English, the native scholars of that language have suggested a structuring of the English sentence into words as follows:

(2) The enemy destroyed the city

This reflects the strong intuitions of the native speaker. (2) is acceptable but not, say: *thee nemy destro yedthe city*, for instance.

If you want to move a little higher in the syntactic hierarchy, the spelling has little help to offer. For instance, the use of the commas:

(3) He wants to see his wife, who lives in Rabat[4]

or

(4) In God, we trust.

This is very inconsistent and sometimes not even used. So we are left with a structure word-by-word as in:

(5) [The] [enemy][destroyed][the][city]

If we rely on the intuition of the native speaker, once more, we can probably achieve much better results. The native speaker would reject intuitively to join *enemy* and *destroyed* as in:

(6) the [enemy destroyed] the city

but he would accept (7) and (8):

(7) [The enemy] destroyed the city

(8) The enemy destroyed [the city]

He would also recognize that *destroyed the city* is a unit of some kind; as it represents the second half of the utterance namely the predicate (in the dichotomy SUBJECT/PREDICATE).

(9) [The enemy] [destroyed the city]

Finally, the whole lot is a unit

(10) [The enemy destroyed the city]

But even now, we would not have exhausted the native speaker's intuitions about the syntactic structure of his language. The native speaker can tell not only which sequences of sounds form a UNIT but also the CATEGORY of each unit. Here we can draw a difference between LEXICAL CATEGORIES: N, V, etc. and PHRASAL CATEGORIES: NP, VP, etc.

The final result of this operation would yield the structure below:

(11)
$[[_{NP}[_{Det}The][_N enemy]][_{VP}[_V destroyed][_{NP}[_{Det}the][_N city]]]]$

What we have obtained has alternatives which are called THREE-DIAGRAM, SYNTACTIC STRUCTURE or a PHRASE-MARKER.

Syntacticians such as Soams and Perlmutter's <u>Syntactic Argumentation and the Structure of English</u> (1979), use TREES, and TRIANGLES as in:

(12)

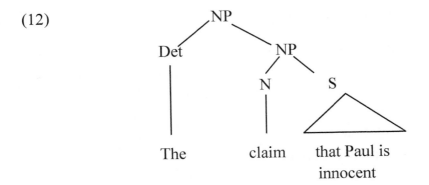

What they seem to be saying with a triangle is: "I am not interested in the internal structure of S above. I will ignore the details, because they are not crucial to my discussion. So unless a bit of the structure is crucial to my present argumentation, I will give it a PARTIAL REPRESENTATION, i.e, a TRIANGLE."

The EST starts on step before S with a bigger unit than the sentence namely S':

(13)

a. S' ----> COMP - S

b. S ----> NP - Aux - VP

etc.

Consider the following sequence:

(14)

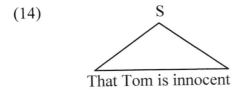

42

Soams & Perlmutter (1979) consider *that Tome is innocent* as an S and *Tom is innocent* is an S, too. To clear this discrepancy, the EST suggests that anything bigger than S is an S':

(15)

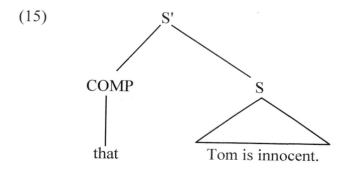

Likewise is Reported Speech:

(16) He asked me [s' whether [s I was happy] *I was happy* is an S. *Whether I was happy* is an S'. S is usually preceded by COMP (such as that, whether, etc.)

1.3.1.2. Empirical arguments

So far we have relied on INTUITION only. To prove that the sentence is indeed structured into a hierarchy, (a successively larger/higher units), let us use a few empirical arguments namely: DISTRIBUTION, INTUSION, COORDINATION, OMISSION and ANAPHORA (See Palmer (1980) or Radford (1981)).

1. DISTRIBUTION: we know that distribution is the main concern of syntax (i.e., the distribution of words within the sentence). Consider the following paradigm (17):

a. [The rich] befriends [the thug] not [the cop]

b. [The cop] befriends [the rich] not [the thug]

c. [The thug] befriends [the cop] not [the rich]

      1   2   3

Let us assume that there are 3 sentences-positions. What we notice about the two words: the and rich, for instance, is that they MOVE TOGETHER to the third and second positions respectively (like two parts of the same body!) We can conclude that our previous intuition about the unit we called Noun Phrase was good.

2. Another argument in favour of units bigger than the word and smaller than the sentence is INTRUSION. Consider the following sentences:

(18)

a. Your comments, I fear, raise more questions than they answer

b. * Your, I fear, comments raise more questions than they solve

(18a) is correct while (18b) is not, which proves that actually *your* and *comments* form a unit.

3. COORDINATION is a third argument in favour of the (intermediary) unit called PHRASE. Consider:

(19)

a. Yesterday, I wrote a letter and a card

b. * Yesterday, I wrote a letter and to John

We notice that acceptability requires coordination to hold not only between units (since *to John* is also a unit namely a **PP**) but requires that the conjoined units should be of the same CATEGORY.

4. The fourth argument concerns OMISSION. Consider the paradigm below:

(20)

a. Paul will wash the dishes but I won't wash the dishes

(20)

a. Paul will wash the dishes but i won't wash the dishes

b.* Paul will wash the dishes but I won't wash the

c.* Paul will wash the dishes but I won't wash

d. Paul will wash the dishes but I won't

In sentence (20d), a VP was omitted; which is indeed a unit.

5. The final argument is called ANAPHORA. It is borrowed from SEMANTICS. It deals with problems of (co)reference (two items referring to the same entity or to two different entities in the real world). Consider the sentence:

(21) I don't like Harry because *the fool* hates linguistics.

(22) [I] , [Harry] and [the fool]

There are two candidates for anaphora with the *fool*; either *I* or *Harry*. To solve this problem let us suggest another sentence:

(23) They don't like Harry because *the fool* hates linguistics.

Because of their clear distinction (plural/singular) we come to the conclusion that *Harry* is coreferential with *the fool* and that *the* and *fool* form one NP unit.

1.3.1.3. Family Relations

If we consider the classical P-Marker once more:

(24)

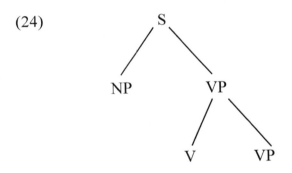

The syntacticians talk – metaphorically – about its NODES: S-node, VP-node, NP-node, etc. like a net.

(25)

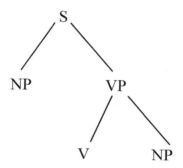

They also like to consider it as (an up-side-down)
TREE, that has BRANCHES:

(26)

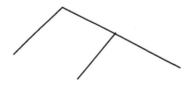

One of the obvious syntactic relations is
PRECEDENCE which is equivalent to the horizontal
relation. That is to say, one item precedes another in a
linear order 1, 2, 3, etc.

(27) The enemy destroyed the city

     1   2   3   4 5

We can also talk about the LEFT and the RIGHT of the
P-Marker:

(28)

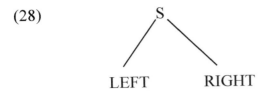

S

LEFT   RIGHT

As a hierarchy (alas!), it has a TOP and a (BOTTOM).
So the syntacticians talk about one node
DOMINATING another. So S dominates all the other
nodes below it.

(29)

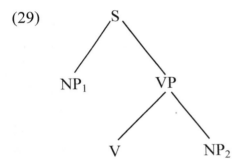

S

NP$_1$ VP

V   NP$_2$

One has to notice that both S and VP dominate NP$_2$.
There is IMMEDIATE DOMINANCE between VP and
NP$_2$ and (simple) DOMINANCE between S and NP$_2$.

Finally, the syntacticians like sometimes to make a
change. They call the sentence a FAMILY (an
exclusively feminist family!). They refer to MOTHERS,
SISTERS and DAUGHTERS. So S is the mother of all
nodes (NP$_1$, VP, V, NP$_2$). NP$_1$ and V are sisters. NP$_1$
and V are daughters of S.

In the early seventies, X-BAR SYNTAX was suggested.
Consider the phrase: *This very fast car*. PS Grammar
would assign the following P-Marker to it:

(30)

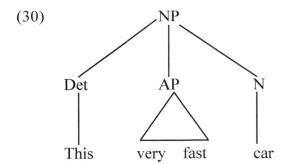

The above tree-diagram claims that this NP has three distinct units:

(31)

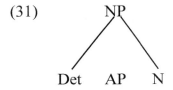

In other words, the sequence AP and N do not form a unit.

An alternative hypothesis would say that *this very fast car* has the following P-Marker:

(32)

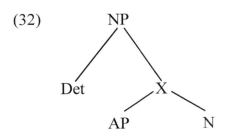

So we are left with two competing hypotheses:

(33)

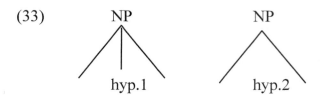

NP   NP

hyp.1   hyp.2

to choose between the two, one can use ANAPHORA once again. Consider the sentence:

(34) I like this very fast car but not that one.

We notice that there is a structural ambiguity; this suggests that we have two cars. We know that one is fast, but we only know that there is another car; we have no idea about its speed possibilities or limitations (35)

The second interpretation is that both are speedy, but like one and do not like the other.

If we stick is the second interpretation, we must admit that one is anaphoric with [very fast car]; in which case we logically have to admit that the three words very, fast and car make one unit. Therefore hypothesis 2 is the correct one.

(37)

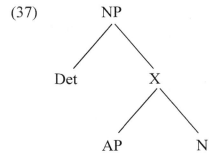

But then we will face the problem of determining the category of X. One plausible answer to this is to say that it is an NP.

(38)

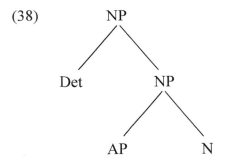

Its distribution is as follows:

(39).

a. I drove this very fast car

b. * I drove very fast car

c. This very fast car is mine

d. *very fast car is mine

Its distribution is neither that of an NP nor that of an N (as it includes other items beside *car*).

It must be an INTERMEDIARY category between NP and N. Hence, the need for X-bar syntax which allows such diversity, as in (40):

(40) X^n must immediately dominate X^{n-1}.

It establishes the following hierarchy theoretically:

(41) $$X^3$$
$$X^2$$
$$X^1$$
$$X^0$$

More practically, it suggests a representation as in (42):

(42) $$X''$$
$$X'$$
$$X$$

(where X is the lexical category itself (N,V, etc.), X' the intermediary category and X" the phrase).

Returning to the phrase *this very fast car* we may suggest structure (43):

(43)

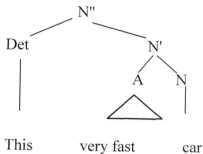

This   very fast   car

1.3.2. Lexicon

Since "Remarks on Nominalization" (1970), the LEXICON has become the focus at the expense of TRANSFORMATIONS. Consider the behavior of verbs such as *put*: *Put* is a verb. It has its own "personality", i.e., SUBCATEGORIZATION:

(44). * I <u>Put</u>

(44) is undergrammatical for lack of a sister. Now if we provided a sister such as *the car*, would this solve the problem?

(45) * I put   the car

It does not. It may need another sister, as in sentence (46):

(46) * I put the car the book

No good! Try and give it a PP denoting LOCATION:

(47)* I put the car in the room.

Still, not good enough since the INTENSION of the word *room* is by definition a place different from a *garage*; i.e., bearing furniture, small door, etc. So the right answer would be:

(49) I put the car in the garage.

Now try and do the same with *give*. Consider the following data:

(50)

a.* He gave

b.* He gave a book

c.* He gave a book at twelve

d.* He gave a book at Mary

e. He gave a book to Mary

So *give* is a verb requiring two sisters: an NP and a (special) PP – namely [to NP]. Consider (51):

(51) ! He gave a book to the wall.

This would require a further refinement concerning SELECTIONAL RESTRICTIONS. The second NP should be [+ human] like *Mary*. But consider (60):

(52) I gave milk to the cat

It seems that [+ human] is too specific (or REDUDUNDANT); [+ animate] is enough. We can formulate the context of the verb *give*, or in the technical jargon its SUBCATEGORIZATION, as follows:

(53) give: V + [--- NP to [NP]]

[+ animate]

The EST proposes a more sophisticated lexicon than the Standard theory. Consider the following data:

(54)

-ly

nice   rude   blanche   grise   rouge

national

nicely   rudely   real

-ise

nationalize

We should first notice that it is made of items taken from two different languages- namely French and English.

(55) FRENCH   ENGLISH

blanche   nice   rude   -ly   -
ise

grise   national moral

rouge   nicely   rational
polite

                               nationalise   rudely
real

Then, we should notice certain patterns:

(56)

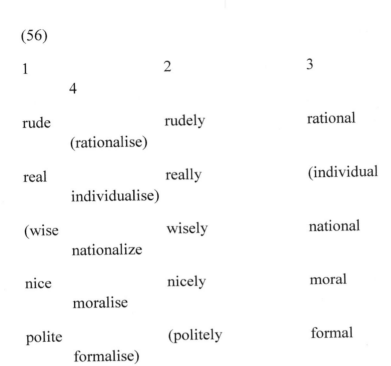

1		2	3
	4		
rude		rudely	rational
	(rationalise)		
real		really	(individual
	individualise)		
(wise		wisely	national
	nationalize		
nice		nicely	moral
	moralise		
polite		(politely	formal
	formalise)		

(57)

a. These are 4 paradigms that can be divided into two sets: the ones containing Adjectives and Adverbs and the ones compromising Adjectives and Verbs.

b. There is a difference between the adjectives in the first set and those in the second —namely those of the second set all end in –al.

c. We notice the parallelism *rude* ⟵ ~~rudely~~, etc. We should be able to capture GENERALIZATION (58):

(58)

a. MORPHOLOGY

$[_{ADJ}X]$ $\longleftrightarrow$ $[_{ADV}[_{ADJ}] -ly]$

b. SEMANTICS: "in the X manner"

($\longleftrightarrow$ stands for LEXICAL Rule)

This is illustrated in (59):

(59)

a. He spoke rudely

b. He spoke in the rude manner

Another type of rule suggested by the EST, concerning the lexicon, is called RESTRURING RULES (Soams & Perlmutter 1979). Consider the following paradigms:

(60)

a. The boy hit the ball

b. The ball was hit by the boy

(61)

a. I go to school

b. * School is gone (by me)

(62)

a. Paul took advantage of the people.

b. The people were taken advantage of.

If we consider sentences (60a,b) on the one hand and sentences (61a,b) on the other hand, we can formulate a first hypothesis saying: "Only OBJECTS of VERBS (by opposition to OJECTS of PREPOSITIONS) can PASSIVIZE".

(63) Hyp. 1: V Object **can**   PASSIVIZE

      P Object **cannot** PASSIVIZE

(60) and (61) further suggest that:

(64) Hyp. 2: TRANSITIVE V   **can** PASSIVIZE

       INTRANSITIVE V **cannot** PASSIVIZE

Hypothesis (2), however, falls against two stumbling blocks. First, there are well-known examples in which TRANSITIVE verbs do not passivize like:

(65)

a. bananas cost £2

b. * 2£ are cost by bananas

We may agree on hypothesis 1. But still the latter poses a problem?

Joan Bresnan (one of Chomsky's students) suggested what she called a RESTRUCTING RULE:

(66)

a. take advantage of NP

b. [v take] [N advantage] [P of] [NP]

(66a) has structure (66b) in which case the NP is the object of a preposition that cannot passitivize.

But we know that sentences such as *The people were taken advantage* of is perfectly acceptable. Bresnan suggests that take advantage of NP should be restricted as follows:

(67) [vGROUP took advantage of] NP

The sequence *took advantage* of is now considered as some kind of Verb Group which allows us to passivize.

(68) V Object **can** PASSIVIZE

Indeed, *take advantage of* can actually be replaced by a verb like *betrayed, decided*, etc.

(69) Paul betrayed the people

Finally, some linguistic such as Jackendoff (1979) have suggested that the Lexicon should include semantic information, viz. THEMATIC RELATIONS. Consider the following paradigm:

(70)

a. The window broke

b. The window was broken

c. I broke the window

d. I broke the window with a hammer

We wonder who is the doer of the action *window, I* or *hammer*.

One can easily notice the discrepancy between the syntactic structure (Subject- V- Object) and the Semantic Structure (Doer of the Action-Action-Victim of the Action.) The subject is not always the doer of the action (sometimes it is the victim of the action) and hence the need for a more adequate and independent terminology to describe the semantic roles played by the different NPs (ARGUMENTS) surrounding a V:

... (71) NP....V   NP...NP

What Jackendoff and others have suggested is as follows:

(72)

a. THEME: The entity that undergoes the action (victim).

b. AGENT: The doer of the action.

We have also GOAL, SOURCE, INSTRUMENT...

So in (72) *window* is the THEME in all four sentences. I is the AGENT and hammer is the INSTRUMENT.

According to IBNSAID, verbs denoting ACTION need FIVE   ARGUMENTS   (at   least):   AGENT-VICTIM/THEME- TIME- SPACE and REASON as in:

(73) Yesterday, he took the train from London King's Cross to Edinburgh

(74)

AGENT: *He*

THEME: *train*

TIME: *yesterday*

SPACE: *London King's Cross*

REASON: *to go to Ebinburgh*

1.3.3. Movements

The movements suggested in the EST subsume previous transformations such as QUESTION, PASSIVE, etc.

Following Soams and Perlmutter (1979), we will assume that Movement rules have the following properties:

(75)

a. "there is a gap somewhere in the sentence and an 'extra constituent" somewhere else.

b. The "extra-constituent" bears the semantic relations it would have if it had started out in the gap.

c. There must have been a constituent in the gap at some stage of the derivation in order, for some transformation, to apply.

Consider the following paradigm:

(76)

a. In God, we trust.

b. The man whom I   met in the hospital

c. Which man did you meet   in the hospital?

d. Which book did I give   to Mary?

e. John, I saw   yesterday at the movies.

We notice that (in addition to the GAP and the extra NP or PP on the LEFT of the sentence) the above sentences pose a serious problem for categorization. As we saw a verb like *give* requires (necessarily) two sisters: an NP and a PP, but in sentence (76d), for instance, it has only the PP.

The solution suggested in Chomsky (1977) is a double fold hypothesis saying:

(77)

a. There is a D-STRUCTURE in which all sub-categorization conditions are fulfilled.

b. There is a MOVEMENT rule which subsequently takes an item from its original position (usually post-verbal position leaving a GAP behind. So as far as Sentence (77d) is concerned we posit: (77) The D-Structure:

I gave which book to Mary?

and then:

A Movement rule –named WH-MOVEMENT would take the NP [which book] to the initial position of the sentence leaving a gap behind:

(78) Which book did I give   to Mary?

Chomsky (1977) assumes that a transformational rule leaves a trace. He also regards the relation between a moved phrase and its trace as essentially one of bound anaphora.

(79)

a. * Bill seems [John to like t]

b. * Bill expected [Mary to like himself]

1.3.4. Constraints

Chomsky had previously suggested what he called the A-OVER-A principle. We may call it the X-OVER-X principle, i.e. any category including another category of the same type within itself does not allow the movement of the smaller Category as in: *I was on my way to school* which presents a PP: to *school* included within a bigger (or HIGHER hence OVER) PP: *on my way to school*. The smaller PP: *to school* cannot be preposed.

The constraints (on the Movement rules) were first discovered and presented by John Ross in his excellent Ph.D dissertation. He called them metaphorically ISLAND CONSTRAINTS. (If you are caught on an island like Alcatraz, you are stuck there!)

WH-ISLAND CONSTRAINTS

(80).... X.. [s.. [s..Y..]]

No movement transformation can extract a constituent out of a relative clause.

(81)

a. The old man [who ran the Marathon] is waiting for the bus

b. * What the old man [who ran?] is waiting for the bus?

Chomsky (1977) suggests a few CONDITIONS ON TRANSFORMATIONS that may supersede Ross'[5] constraints, such as TENSED S CONDITION, SENTENTIAL SUBJECT CONDITION and SUBJACENCY.

TENSED S CONDITION:

No transformational rule can involve X and Y in structures of type (a), where S-bar is tensed:

(82)

a. .. X [$_{S'}$.. Y..]

b. * John seems [that t likes Bill]

SENTENTIAL SUBJECT CONDITION

No constituent can be moved out of a sentential subject (i.e., out of a clause which is itself the subject of another clause):

(83) * Tomorrow [for him to leave t] would be a pity

SUBJACENCY

No constituent can be moved out of more that one containing NP or S node (in any single movement rule):

(84) * Mary is thought [John to want [t to win]]

The cycle can play down Subjacency, as seen in (85) in which COMP is the safe-conduct:

(85) who$_1$ did [you say [$_{COMP}$ t1 [he saw t$_1$]]

Notes

1. TRACE THEORY (which Joseph Aoun and Fiengo like to call REST i.e., Revised Extended Standard Theory)

2. X-BAR SYNTAX is also used by the GAZDAR whom English like to consider as a challenge to Chomsky. He uses X-BAR SYNTAX and PRAGMATICS.

3. Kenya not-be problematic; i.e. Kenya has got no problems.

4. Restrictive vs Descriptive relative clauses (cf. Appendix)

5. Ross's Conditions on transformations were a sharp reduction of the potential rules and thereby an extraordinary move towards explanatory adequacy and a reduction of the number of competing grammars available to language learners. (Riemdijk & Williams 1986)

1.4. Government and Binding

1.4.1. GB Principles and Parameters1

According to Langacker (1969), the goal of linguistic theory is to state the major conditions on (different transformations such as) PRONOMINALIZATION. He suggests who constraints, viz., COMMAND and PRECEDE as crucial in this respect. These allow a considerable simplification of the grammar as they represent a long step towards limiting the scope of this transformation. The question he poses is: "when can we pronominalize a second NP?"

COMMAND is defined as: "a node A 'commands' another node B if neither A nor B dominates the other; and the S-node that most immediately dominates A also dominates B".

The major conditions on pronominalization will be as follows: NP_1 may pronominalize NP_2 unless NP_2 precedes NP_1; and NP_2 commands NP_1.

(1)

a. John saw John

b. John thinks John is clever

In (1a,b) John can pronominalize (i.e., function as the antecedent of) the second occurrence of John as it precedes and commands it.

(2)

a. John is much more intelligent than he looks

b. Tell that man that he can't go in there

In (2) NPs *John* and *that man* precede and command he. They may be interpreted as coreferential.

According Chomsky (1981), U.G. consists of the following interacting systems of rules.

(3)

a. Lexicon

b. Categorial component and Transformational component

c. PF component

d. LF component

The lexicon would state, among other things, the subcategorization of verbs. A verb like promise will be followed by NP and either S' or NP:

(4) *promise* $\begin{Bmatrix} \text{NP} & \text{S'} \\ \text{NP} & \text{NP} \end{Bmatrix}$

The categorical and Transformational components are context free and context sensitive respectively. They operate as follows:

(5)

a. A →B   C

b. 1   2   3 → 3 2 1

(5b) can be exemplified in French causatives:

(6) Je ferais Jean téléphone à ses parents→   Je ferais
téléphoner John à ses parents

The PF component includes transformations such as
(American) *wanna* contraction:

(7) want to →wanna

The LF representation of a sentence such as *John seems to
be sad* is either (8) following STANDARD LOGIC:

(8) seems (sad (John))

Sad is the predicate of *John* and *seems* is the predicate of
the complex subject sad John or (7) following Binding
theory:

(9) John $_1$ [seems [t$_1$ to be sad]]

According to Chomsky (1982) the alternative would be to
substitute a system of PRINCIPLES & PARAMETERS to
the above system of rules. These principles are the
following (they will be discussed in turn):

(10)

a. X-bar theory

b. θ-theory

c. Case theory

d. Binding theory

e. Bounding theory

f. Control theory

g. Government theory

1.4.1.1. X-bar theory

Since "Remarks on Nominalization" (1970), Chomsky has suggested an alternative to PS grammar (see 1.1.); namely X-bar theory. It would deal with the structure of different constituents in a more adequate fashion. It would especially refer to the intermediate order between the PHRASE and the HEAD (X). The latter is an essential syntactic unit. It affects the whole phrase and gives it its main characteristics.

The new rules are as follows:

(11)

a. X' ———→ X..

b. X" ———→ [Spec, X']   X'

c. S ———→ N"   V"

Developing this idea further, Sells (1985) suggests the following configuration of constituents:

(12)

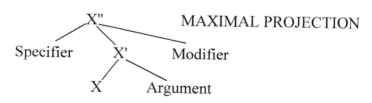

The above structure means that any constituent is composed of a HEAD. So for instance, the noun is the head of the noun phrase (and the part that gives it its nouniness). The verb is the head of the verb phrase, etc. The head has sisters which are called ARGUMENTS.

The head plus the argument form the intermediary order (between the head and the phrase) which is X'. It is surrounded by SPECIFIER (i.e., determiner) and MODIFIER (i.e., adjectives).

The phrase is the MAXIMAL PROJECTION of the head (X"). The maximal projections are N" V", P", A", S' (X").

An argument is any constituent that serves as the sister of the head (the part that the head governs, see below).

So, X-bar theory would represent the noun phrase *the false claim that Paul was innocent* as follows:

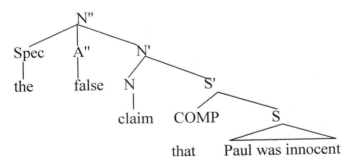

Likewise, in (14a) the head is *proud*, the complement is PP *of John* while the specifier is missing. In (14b) the head is *pictures*, the specifier is *the* and the complement is PP *of John*.

(14)

a. proud of John

b. The pictures of John

1.4.1.2. ө-theory

ө-theory relies on the semantic knowledge of the native speaker. It has to do with the different semantic roles played by the different NPs surrounding the predicate. A verb such as *give*, for instance, has three main ө-roles which are: THEME, AGENT, BENEFACTIVE (cf. Lyons 1977).

(15)

a. John gave the book to Mary

b. Tom rolled the ball down the hill to the river

In (15a) *John* is agent, the *book* is theme and *Mary* is benefactive. In (15b) *Tom* is agent, *the ball* is theme, *the hill* is source and *the river* is goal.

1.4.1.3. Case theory

Case theory is an abstract notion (in English at least) which suggests that no phonetic NP (by opposition to empty NPs) can remain without case. Case is most overly expressed in English with pronouns:

(16) They gave them back their book

(17) * Them gave their back they book

(18) * Him will see he

Sells (1985) notice that only personal pronouns have retained their case distinctions in Modern English. For example, *they* is nominative, *them* objective (or accusative) and their genitive. (For the principles of CASE see 1.4.4). Case assignment is subject to case filter.

CASE FILTER

(19) * NP, if NP has phonetic content and no case.

Considering ditransitives, Sells (1985) notices that if only the first NP gest case from the verb, then only it should be forced to move in passive:

(20)

a. We gave Mary the book

b. * We gave the book Mary

c. Mary was given the book

d.* The book was given Mary

The above examples show that it is the GOAL argument that must follow the verb. The last two examples show that only this NP can passivize.

1.4.1.4. Bonding theory

Binding theory is concerned with the semantic relations that link the different NPs of a sentence between them and ultimately link them to entities in the real world. Binding theory requires:

(21)

a. X GOVERNS Y

b. X and Y are COINDEXED

c. An inclusive GOVERNING CATEGORY (GC) such as NP or S

d. Every NP in the sentence must be either FREE or BOUND.

Binding theory characterizes the imperative relations of NPs, and partitions the class of nominal into three types.

Binding Conditions:

(22)

a. An anaphor is bound in its governing category

b. A pronominal is free in its governing category

c. An R-expression is free

(23)

a. John told Bill about him

b. They wanted each other to win

c. John thinks he is clever

d. Who did you say t [he saw t]^2

e. Les soldats se tuent

f. Les soldats se rasent

In (23a) *him* is a pronominal; it must be free in its GC. So it will refer to a third person, rather than *John* or *Bill*. In (23b) each other is a reciprocal. It is bound to *they*. In (23c) *he* is either coreferential with *John* or free. In (23e) the anaphor *se* is bound and furthermore has a GROUP interpretation, i.e., the soldiers, as a group, are killing the other soldiers as a group, whereas in (23f) it has a DISTRIBUTIVE one, i.e., each individual is shaving himself.

The trace (or variable) in (23d) is similar to anaphors in what concerns binding (coindexing) and governing category. The wh-item has CROSSED-OVER the pronoun. It cannot be understood as anaphoric with any of the pronouns that c-command it. It behaves like an R-expression.

(24)

a. Who did he think that he said [he saw t]

b. ?x_1 [x_1: a person] he thinks that he said he saw x_1

c. Who did he think that Bill$_2$ saw x_1

1.4.1.5. Bounding theory

Bounding theory has to do with the landing site of MOVE ALPHA. You can move items around but there are limitations to that (as well as to their interpretation). To move from d-structure to s-structure (or LF), you apply move alpha which is subject to BOUNDING (i.e., SUBJACENCY).

(25) ---- seems [$_s$ John want [$_s$ Mary to win]]

In (25), we have two potential candidates for move alpha; either *John* or *Mary*. If we move *John* to the initial position, we obtain grammatical sentence (26a), whereas moving Mary results in ungrammatical sentence (26b):

(26)

a. John seems t to want Mary to win

b. * Mary seems John to want t to win

The reason for this is that *John* had to cross only one boundary; the S-node containing *want*, whereas Mary has to cross two boundaries; the S containing want and the S containing *win*. This is forbidden by Bounding theory.

Now, there is a difference between NP-movement and WH-movement (both being instances of move alpha). WH-movement would move an item from an A-position (with θ and case) to an A-bar position without θ nor case. NP movement is different as it moves items from an A-position to another A-position. Consider (27):

(27)

a. [[The city]₁ was destroyed [t]₁]

b. [What]₁ did [you say [t]₁]

We call a CHAIN the set composed of the moved item and its trace (ȧ,t). The trace is an empty category. It receives a θ-role but no case by opposition to ALPHA which has case but no θ-role.

1.4.1.6. Control theory

Control theory is a subtheory of Binding. It "is concerned with the choice of antecedents for PRO". PRO is neither a pronoun nor a preform. It is an empty category (like t and pro).

In a sentence like *they want to live forever*; the second verb live does not seem to have a subject (any overt subject, at least). We say that its subject is PRO; a phonetically empty category.

(28)They want PRO to live for ever

Control theory has to do with syntax but also involves semantics and infers on pragmatics. There are two types of control verbs (or predicates): OBLIGATORY CONTROL as in verbs like want and adjectives like eager and ARBITRARY CONTROL as in (29b).

(29) a. John is eager [PRO to please]

b. [PRO to jog] on the main street is unhealthy

In (29a) the antecedent (or controller) of PRO is the subject of the matrix clause John, whereas in sentence (29b) PRO can refer to *me*, *someone*, people in general. It is a case of arbitrary control.

1.4.1.7. Government theory

To understand the notion GOVERNMENT one has to talk three notions at least). The three notions involved here are notion GOVERNOR, the notion GOVERNEE and the notion GOVERNING CATEGORY.

(30) X governs Y if:

a. Every maximal projection dominating X dominates Y (so X is the governor and Y the governee)

b. The governing category for Y is the smallest NP or S containing (i.e., dominating) Y and a governor of Y.

Subcategorization, case, binding and θ-marking are assigned under government. A verb for instance cannot subcategorize for an NP in another clause. The domain of a head is its maximal projection and government can be equated with subcategorization. Government is equated with C-COMMAND. Consider the tree below:

(31)a.

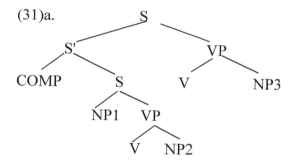

b. That John likes bananas   amazes   me

In (31a,b), we have the following c-command relations:

(32)

a. NP$_1$ c-commands NP$_2$ *true*

b. NP$_1$ c-commands NP$_3$ *false*

c. NP$_2$ c-commands NP$_1$ *false*

d. NP$_2$ c-commands NP$_3$ *false*

e. NP$_3$ c-commands NP$_1$ *false*

f. NP$_3$ c-commands NP$_2$ *false*

1.4.2. Empty Categories

Chomsky (1982) suggests that there are two types of empty categories TRACE and PRO. Their study is related to that of anaphors and pronouns. They present similar syntactic and semantic properties. Actually a gathering of the two is possible as in (33):

(33)

Overt EC	ANAPHORIC	PRONOMINAL
Pronoun pro	-	+
Reflexive NP trace	+	-
R-expression Wh-trace	-	-
PRO	+	+

Chomsky (1982) further suggests a typology of empty categories that determines the semantic function of ECs from their structural properties:

"*suppose that the EC is locally bound by an element in theta-bar position. Then it is [- pronominal], either [- anaphor] if the local binder is in an A-bar position or*

78

*[+anaphor] if the local binder is in an A-position. (...)
Suppose the EC is free or locally bound by an element in a
theta position. Then it is [+ pronominal], just in the case
of overt category with these properties.. [whereas] the
feature [+ anaphoric] can be selected only in an
ungoverned position. "*

Hence, a theta position is necessarily an A-position but not
the other-way-round. Consider sentences (34):

(34)

a. [I]   know   that   [John]   saw   [Mary]

  Ө   Ө-bar   Ө-bar   Ө   Ө-bar   Ө

  A   A-bar   A-bar   A   A-bar   A

b. [It]   rains

  Ө-bar   Ө-bar

  A   A-bar

c. [$_{COMP}$ The Ireland   that] [I saw   EC]

    Ө-bar   Ө

    A-bar   A

Aoun (1985) suggests four possibilities, since anaphors are
characterized with respect to their antecedents, as follows:

(35)

     ANTECEDENT   ANAPHOR

A	A	
reflexices, NP trace		
A	A-bar	l'uno
in Italian		
A-bar	A	wh-
trace, trace of clitics		
A-bar	A-bar	traces
in COMP		

An instance of an anaphor in an A-bar position can be found in reciprocals in Italian. Reciprocals are expressed by the discontinuous expression *l'uno...l'atro* (lit. 'the one..the other'). *L'uno*- the antecedent of *latro*- is in an A-position. We need to show that *l'uno* is in a A-bar position. In this respect we notice that *l'uno* is in an A-position.

(36)

a. John$_1$ likes himself$_1$

b. John$_1$ is likely t$_1$ t$_o$ win

c. who did John say that Peter likes t

d. l'umo ammira le foto dell'altro

one admires your pictures of the other

1.4.3. CP/IP Barriers

In Chomsky (1986b), there is a further sophistication of X-bar theory which is formulated as follows:

(37)

a. X' = X   X"*

b. X" = X"*   X'

as in (38) [$_{X''}$ the [$_{X'}$ [$_X$ car] of the boss]]]

Which is then generalized to encapsulate non-lexical categories such as I and C:

(39)

a. The boy [$_I$ will] hit the ball

b. man [$_C$ llaəii] kaan-a ya -lcbu

who that   was-3sm 3sm –play

In (39) I will is the head of the IP (=S). In (39b) C llaəii is the head of CP (=S'). Move Alpha is then based on the triology suggested in X-bar; namely HEAD, COMPLEMENT and SPECIFIER, as follows:

(40)

a. There is no movement to complement position

b. Only X can move to the head position

c. Only X" can move to the specifier position

d. X and X" are "visible" to move alpha

These are respectively exemplified in (41)

(41)

a. * t₁ was destroyed the enemy ₁

b. The enemy –ed destroy the city ⟶

the enemy   destroyed t_v the city

c. [CP[NP which car] did he put   t in the garage

d. * [N' big city] was destroyed the

Barrierhood is an attempt to unify those categories that move alpha and those that prevent government as in

(42)

a. * Mary ₁ seems John to want   t₁ to win

b. * I know [[him will come]]

Alternatively one (or more) maximal projections, Subjancency, Blocking Categories and Minimal Distance are used as criteria for BARRIERHOOD:

(43)

a. I know him

b. * I want he will go

c. * I know him will go

The ungrammatically of (43c) is alternatively explained in terms of Barrierhood. The verb *know* cannot govern him as there is a barrier CP (that-clause) preventing it from doing so. The alternative being in terms of minimality, *him*, has a closer (viz minimal) governor in TNS *will* of the embedded clause.

Following May (1985), Chomsky (1986) suggests some of the LF properties of QR support VP adjunction as in (44):

(44)

a. Who does [$_{VP}$ everyone [$_{VP}$ like   t]

In (44) either *who* or *everyone* may have WIDER SCOPE. QR will adjoin the quantifier to IP

(45) Who$_1$ does [$_{IP}$ everyone $_2$ [IP t$_2$ like t$_1$]

DOMINANCE is redefined as follows:

Node X dominates A only if the two

SEGEMENTS of X dominate A, as in (46):

(46) C [$_X$..B [$_X$..A..]

C is excluded, i.e., not dominated by node X.

In (46) X dominates A. It does not dominate B and X excludes C.

LOGICAL FORM (Quantifier Raising in particular) is said to use these notions to deal with ambiguous sentences as in (47):

(47)

a. Who $_2$ [$_{IP}$ everyone [$_{IP}$ x likes x]

b. Everyone [who [x likes x]

In (47a) say the Queen, is referred to by *who* (which c-commands and) has WIDER SCOPE. In (47b) there is a difference a person in each case. *Everyone* has wider scope.

1.4.4. Cliticization

Among the major works done on clitics within the Chomskyan GB framework, Borer (1989), Kayne (1987) and Ouhalla (1989). This chapter aims at giving a universal grammar of cliticization based on works such as Chomsky (1981, 1986b and 1988). It basically refutes previous assumptions such as Kayne's I-lexical marking (1987) and Ouhalla's CPC/swoop fashion (1989). It suggests either a (local) step-by step clitic-movement, or a base generation of clitic/agreement markers.

1.4.4.1. Introduction

Pronominalization has provided generative grammarians with very important insights into the syntax and (co-reference) of pronouns[1] in the '60s and '70s (cf.Langacker (1969), Lasnik (1976), etc.). The clitic pronouns[2] showed even more peculiar behavior in Romance and (Hamito)-Semitic languages. They were alternatively seen as generated at d-structure (cf. Borer (1989)) or derived via move alpha (cf. Kayne (1987) and Ouhalla (1989)). The problems posed by the latter option are as follows:

A. Is clitic movement an odd instance of move alpha, i.e. unconstrained as in Ouhalla's (1989) swoop fashion?

B. In case it is constrained, does it depend on certain features present in some but not all languages such as the richness of the I-nodes as assumed in Kayne (1987)?

C. Is there any possible way of brining clitic movement (all instances) within the scope of the general rule of move alpha?

As a reminder, the G.B. theory assigns each sentence structure derived from a deep structure by a (possibly null) set of applications of the rule called 'move alpha'.

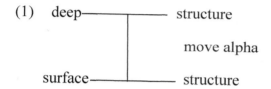

(1) deep—————————— structure

move alpha

surface—————————— structure

Move alpha is a generalization of the previous transformations such as NP movement and Wh-movement (cf. Chomsky's Extended Standard Theory) that came to cover head-movement such as V-movement and Clitic movement:

(2) a. the city was destroyed t_i

b. who$_i$ do you think he saw t_i

c. he open$_i$ -ed t_i the door

d. Jean les$_i$ a vues t_i

'John saw them'

Move alpha is subject to many constraints such as Subjacency[3], the Empty Category Principle (ECP) [4] and Head Movement Condition (HMC)[5] illustrated respectively in (3):

(3) a. * elle$_i$ semble [IP 1 Jean veut que [IP2 t_i gagne]]

she seems   John   wants   that win

b. * tu$_i$ parais que t$_i$ tu as rencontré un ami

you seem that you have met a friend

c. John open$_i$ –ed t$_i$ the door

In (3a) *elle* has crossed two bounding nodes IP1 and IP 2 thus violating the bounding principles of Subjacency. The EPC requires a trace to be properly governed by a lexical item (such as N, V, Adj, P). In (3b), the governor *que* does not count as a proper (lexical) governor for the trace t$_i$ so the ECP. Finally (3c) respects the strict locality requirements of HMC on head-movement.

Case applies after move alpha has applied. It is assumed to have the following fundamental properties (Chomsky 1981, p.170):

(4). a. NP is nominative if governed by AGR[6]

b. NP is objective if governed by V

c. NP is oblique if governed by P

d. NP is genitive in [$_{NP}$-----X']

e. NP is inherently case-marked as determined by properties of its [-N] governor.

These cases can be illustrated in what follows:

(5) il   a donné   [son livre]   à   Marie

NOM.   GEN.   OBLIQUE

[OBJECTIVE]

'he has given his book to Mary'

Each case is assigned by a head governor 7. X, under an X' mother. In the case of the clitics, Borer (1984, p. 34) assumes the following configuration:

(6)

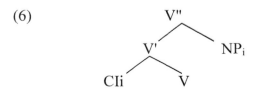

(6) can be generalized to (7) and illustrated in (8):

(7)

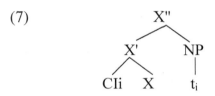

(8) a. Jean [VP   les$_i$ veut   t$_i$]

'John wants them'

b. [NP   kitaabu-hui   t$_i$]

'his book'

1.4.4.2. Kayne's Inflectional –Lexical Marking & Clitic (Long) Movement

1.4.4.2.1. Clitic (long) movement in Romance languages

In Kayne (1987, p.241) clitic movement is considered as a case of head movement. The clitic moves stepwise head-to-head, subject to the HMC. Also when I is rich enough to license null subject it will allow clitic (long) movement.

(9) I-Lexical Marking (ILM): An I that can license a null subject can L-mark its VP complement even if the verb does not move up to it.

(10) a. Parlo Italiano (Italian)

'(I) speak Italian '

b. il parle

'he speaks'

(11) a. Gianni le vuole leggere

John them want-3sm read-to

'John wants to read them'

b. * Jean les veut lire

'John wants to read them'

There is a difference between null subject languages- like Italian- and non-nul subject languages like French – as far as clitic (long) movement is concerned. In Italian I is strong enough to license a null subject, L-Mark VP and consequently allow clitic long movement.

The embedded VP is L-marked by I, as we have said, and the embedded CP is L-marked by the matrix verb. This goes hand in hand with the strict locality requirements of the HMC:

(12)...V [$_{CP}$ [$_{IP}$ I [$_{VP}$]]]

The second claim in Kayne (1987) is that clitic movement operates stepwise as attested by the following structure:

(13) a. Cl$_i$ V [$_{CP}$ t$_i$ [[$_i$

b. Gianni le$_i$ vuole t$_i$ leggere t$_i$

The stepwise fashion is not restricted to clitic movement but includes V-movement as well and is a V-movement to I, then the complex V-I moves to C. This is how the intervening barriers are cleared away for the clitic to be able to climb to the matrix clause (cf. Chomsky 1986, p. 70):

(14)

a. [C [$_{TNSP}$ I [$_{VP}$ V]]]

b. [$_C$ [$_{TNSP}$ V$_i$-I [VP t$_i$]]]

c. [$_C$ Vi [$_{TNSP}$ t$_i$ [VP t$_i$]]]

Once this step-by step V-movement has been achieved, the clitic gets the freedom to cross the two barriers- VP and TNSP- without problem.

Kayne notes, however, that although Italian has got a strong I that can L-mark VP and TNSP and license clitic long movement, this operation is contingent, however, upon an empty C node; because a filled C node will block clitic (long) movement as in (15):

(15) * Non li so se fare

NEG them-know-1s if do-to

'I don't know whether to do them'

In French there is a further snag. Clitic long movement is lexically determined, as suggested by Kayne (1978, p. 242):

(16) Matrix Verb Condition (MVC)[8]: the matrix verb must be compatible with long clitic movement.

(17) a. Marie a fait lire les lettres à Jean

Mary made John read the letters

b. * Je l'ai laissé lire aux enfants

I them-let read to kids

Clitic long movement depends on the nature of the matrix verb. A verb like *faire* allows this operation, while a non-trigger verb like *laisser* would not allow it. This is seen also in the behavior of verbs like *vouloir* (as opposed to *faire*).

(18) a. Je veux qu'il l'écrive à Marie

'I want him to write to Mary'

b. Je la lui fais écrire à Marie

'I make hi mit to Mary'

As far as the embedded verb is concerned, Kayne notes the difference in nature and behavior found between finite and non-finite clauses:

(19) a. Je veux qu'il les lisent

'I want him to read them'

b. Je les fais lire à John

'I made John read them'

Ciltic long movement seems easier with finite embedded verbs.

Finally, Kayne notes the interplay between verb subcategorization and the case of the clitics. French has got different pronominal forms reflecting a specific case each, namely: *il*, *le*, *son* et *lui* which are nominative, objective, genitive and oblique respectively.

(20) Il lui a donné/ son livre

     'he gave it to him/his book'

     NOM. OBJ. OBL.   GEN.

(21)

    a. Il est parti

   'he is gone'

    b. Je l'ai fais partir

   'I made him go'

(22) a. Il l'a lu/ le like

'he read it/the book'

b. Je le lui fais lire

'I made him read it'

In (21a) above *partir* is intransitive, its subject is nominative. When the sentence is causativised the clitic becomes objective. Whereas in sentence (22a) the verb *manger* is transitive, its (nominative) subject turns oblique when causativized while object keeps its objective case.

1.4.4.2.2. Kayne's ILM and Arabic cliticization

Arabic, a staunch null subject language, presumably has an I strong enough to license a null subject and consequently allow, following Kayne, long clitic movement:

(23) jaa?a

(he) came

(24) ?araada ?an yusaafiha-hu

want-3sm to shake-hands-3sm-him

'he wanted to shake hands with him'

Although Arabic is a null subject language as shown in (23), it does not seem to confirm Kayne's ILM.

It could be argued that filled C node (viz *?an*) is responsible for blocking clitic movement.

Faire-like verbs are trigger verbs, as we saw above, and should be expected to behave uniformally across languages:

(25) jaᶜal-tu-hu   yaqra?u-hu

made-1s-him   3sm-read-them

'I made him read them'

In (25) neither the empty node C nor the trigger verb *jacala* 'make' are capable of licensing long clitic movement in Arabic:

The finite/non-finite dichotomy plays very little either in this respect.

We witness rather a case of reconstruction:

(26) a. ?urridu [IP ?an   ?aqra.ahum]

1s-want   to   1s-read-them

'I want to read them'

b. ?uriidu [NP   qiraa?ata-hu]

1s want   reading-their

The clitic remains in its initial position; it is turned from objective case to genitive. The embedded clause is reconstructed as a noun phrase.

Case shift is further noted in Arabic, as illustrated below:

a.   əahab-a

went-he

'he went away'

b. ja^{c}altu-hu   yaəhabu

made- 1s-him   3sm-go

'I made him go'

(28) a. tazawwaj-a-haa

married-3sm-her

'he married her'

c. ja^{c}altu-hu   yatazawwaju-haa

made-1s-him   3sm-married-her

'I made him marry her'

Whether the verb is transitive or intransitive , its subject turns from nominative to objective, when causativized.

1.4.4.3. Ouhalla's CPC/ Swoop Fashion

1.4.4.3.1. Ouhalla's CPC and clitic movement

In "Clitic Movement & the ECP" (1989), Ouhalla defends the ECP (Chomsky 1981, p.250) as opposed to the HMC (Chomsky 1986, p.71). He uses a data from Berber and Romance languages, and suggests his CPC/ swoop fashion as an answer to cliticization:

(29) CPC: Clitics must attach/move to the highest affixal head element in their construction, (general principles of UG (i.e., ECP) allowing) (Ouhalla 1989, p.178).

Ouhalla relies heavily on Kayne (1987). The latter has dealt with the clitics in French and Italian:

(30)

  a. Jean les a lues   t

  'John has read them'

  b. Gianni li vuole   t verdere   t

  'John wants to see them'

The objective clitic *les* moves to the (pre) INFL position, leaving the agreement marker *–es* (feminine, plural) attached to the verb *lu*. In Italian the operation is more interesting as it takes the objective clitic *li* (stepwise according to Kayne and in one swoop according to Ouhalla) from the embedded clause to the matrix clause. Kayne suggests that this (long) clitic movement is made possible by the fact that I is lexical in Italian- a null subject language (as seen above).

Ouhalla relies on Berber (Northern dialect) which a null subject language to defend his CPC.

(31)   yussad

    came (he)

'he came'

(32)   ad-t   ya-rzam / tawwart

         will-it   3sm-open / door

         'he will open the door / it'

Following Kayne (1987), I in Berber should be strong enough to L-mark VP and consequently licence clitic (long) movement in one swoop according to Ouhalla (1989, p. 174).

His CPC analysis faces; however, many clear counterexamples from various languages, including Berber itself. Ouhalla (1989, p. 182) notes the optional character of PCl movement in his own dialect:

(33) a. ad   y-arzam   tawwart   asg-as

        will-3sm-open   door   with-it

        'he will open the door with it'

     b. ad-sa-as   y-arzam tawwart

        will-with-it   3sm open door

        'he will open the door with it'

In causatives, Berber- a morphological language- hardly allows the biclausal structure that would permit (or hinder) clitic long movement (Ouhalla 1989, p. 198):

(34) a. ss-idf-n Ali

         cause-enter-3p Ali

'they made Ali enter'

b. ss-idf-nt

cause-enter-3p-him

'they made him enter'

In Eastern Berber, CPC simply does not apply (Khaddouma, p.c.):

(35) a. xadi y-arzzam   ?akid-at θawwarə

will 3s-open with-it door

'he will open the door with-it'

b. xadi y-razzam-s ?akid l-maftah

will 3s-open-it with the key

'he will open it with the key'

In (35a) Cl movement is naught and in (35b) objective clitic movement is to the nearest head *razzam* 'open' rather than to the highest head *xadi* 'will', as predicted by Ouhalla's CPC.[9]

1.4.4.3.2. CPC and Head-movement

Ouhalla tries to generalize his CPC from clitic to head movement, namely V-movement, and from Berber to Universal Grammar:

(36)

a. Les garçons ecri-r-ont les lettres

'the boys will write the letters'

b. Les garçons les écrivent

'the boys will write them'

c....AGR   TNS   V   Cl

Suppose that the d-structure of (36b) is (36c), if we follow Ouhalla's CPC/one-swoop fashion we would obtain the following s-structure:

(37)

a. Cl$_j$ V^i AGR   TNS   t$_i$ t$_j$

b. *... les écri-ont-r

This is a result which is far undesirable.

A more plausible derivation would be reached step-by-step as follows:

(38)

a.... AGR   TNS   V   Cl

b. V- TNS

c. [V-TNS]- AGR

d. [V- TNS- AGR]   Cl

c. [Cl-V- TNS- AGR]

f.... les écri-r-ont

1.4.4.3.3. Ouhalla's CPC/swoop fashion and move alpha

To generalize the CPC from head-movement (wiz. CL movement) to 'move alpha' would be even less successful. The CPC (?) would force a long direct NP/Wh-movement to the initial position of the sentence:

(39)

    a. * Mary seems John to want   t   to win

    b. John seems   t   to want Mary to win

(40)

    a. * Who did you say that   t   saw John

    b. Who did you say   t   saw John

(41)

    a. * The city seems the enemy destroyed   t

    b. The city seems   t   to be destroyed

By opposition to Ouhalla's CPC, the step-by-step fashion- like Subjacency- is based on a strict locality condition. In (39a) *Mary* has crossed two boundaries (the *want* and *win* clauses) violating Subjacency. In (39b) John has crossed one step (namely the *want* clause). In (40a) the presence of the complementizer that prevents the step-by-step locality, while its absence in (40b) allows it. Finally, in (41a) the *city* has moved directly from the object position of the destroy- clause to the initial position violating the step-by-step fashion, while (41b) respects the locality condition; the *city* moves first to the subject position of the embedded clause before moving to the subject position of the matrix clauses; as in (42):

(42) a. _____ seems the enemy destroyed the city

b. _____ seems the city was destroyed

c. the city seems   t   to be destroyed   t

1.4.4.4. The Clitics according to the Traditional Arab Grammarians

1.4.4.4.1. Case

Case plays a crucial role in Arabic grammar and could be summarized as follows:

A. Nominative

a. Subject (or Inchoative)

jaa?a ʃ-ʃitaa?u

came the-winter

'winter came'

?aʃ-ʃitaa?u jaa?a

b. Enuniciative

?aʃ-ʃitaa?u qaadimun

the-winter coming

'winter is coming'

B. Oblique

a. A noun governed by a preposition

?ila l-jaami^{c}ati

'to the university'

b. Annexation

qalamu   t-taalibi

pen the-student

'the pen of the student'

C. Objective

All the nouns are objective

(El Halwani, p.c.)

1.4.4.4.2. The Clitics

1.4.4.4.2.1. The case of the clitics

Clitics are subject to case as illustrated below:

(44)

a. jaa?a-t-i- t-taalibaatu[10]

came-3pf the student-3pf

'the students came'

b. zaara-hu Ali

visited-3sm-him Ali

'Ali visited him'

c. kitaabu-hu

book-his

'his book'

d. min-hu

from-him

'from him'

In (44a) -t is a nominative clitic subject of jaa?a 'he came'. In (44b) -hu is an objective clitic object of *zaara* 'he visited'. In (44c) -hu is a genitive clitic annexed to kitaabu 'book'. And finally, in (44d) -hu is an oblique clitic governed by min 'from'.

1.4.4.4.2.2. The Returning clitic

The Returning clitic shows up in qualitative constructions and falls back upon some antecedent as in:

(45) a. Ali ?ibnu-hu hasanun

Ali son-his handsome

'Ali's son is handsome'

b. Zaid maata ?abuu-hu

Zaid died -3sm father-his

'Zaid's father died'

c. Khalid jii?a ?ilaj-hi bi-kitaabin

102

Khalid came to-him with book-a

'a book has been brought to Zaid'

In (45a) the generative clitic –hu refers back to *Ali*. In (45b) the genitive clitic *–hu* falls back upon *Zaid*. In (45c) the oblique clitic refers to *Khalid*. In all three cases the antecedent of the returning clitic (*?ar-raabit* 'the Binder') is an enunciative.[11]

The Returning clitic shows up in questions also, as illustrated in:

(46) man bi-jadi-hi   malakuutu kulli ʃaj?

who in-hands-his kingdom- a everything

'In Whose hands is the kingdom over everything' (Wright 1979)

The interrogative *man* 'who' is put in the nominative absolute and its proper place is supplied by the returning clitic –hi which falls back upon it.[12]

1.4.4.4.2.3. Nominative clitics

Traditional Arab grammarians did not overlook the nominative clitic. Wright (1979, p.55) suggests the following table as a general classification for them:

(47) suffixed nominative pronouns:

SINGULAR

	MAS.	COMMON	FEM.
3p			-t
2p	-ta		-ti
1p		-tu	

DUAL

	MAS.	COMMON	FEM.
3p	-aa		-taa
2p		-tumaa	
1p			

PLURAL

	MAS.	COMMON	FEM.
3p	-uu	(na)	-na
2p	-tum		-tunna
1p		-naa	

(ibid, pp. 256-314)

However, this table leaves a few loopholes and discrepancies[13]. A more consistent classification would be as in (48):

(48)

	MASCULINE		FEMININE
	SING.		
1p	-tu	-tu	-tu

104

2p	-ta	-ta	-ti
3p		-a	-at

DUAL

1p		
2p	-tumaa	-tumaa
3p	-aa	-ataa

PLURAL

1p	-naa	-naa
2p	-tum	-tunna
3p	-uu (na)	-na

1.4.4.4.3. Agreement

1.4.4.4.3.1. Noun-follower agreement (?ism-taabic)

While Chomsky (1986, p.13) considers Head-Specifier agreement (as between subject and I) to be an essential grammatical relation, traditional Arab grammarians dealt essentially with ?ism-taabic 'noun follower' agreement following what they referred to as 4/10 Ratio أربعة من عشر illustrated in (50):

(49) John work-s

(50) a. rajulun kariimun   INDEFINITE

      man-a generous-a

      'a generous man'   SING. (see Minimalist Program)

1.4.4.4.3.2. The returning clitic agreement

The clitic, in the qualificative clause, agrees with its antecedent in person at least, as shown in (51):

(51) a. marartu bi-man yu-hibbuka

      passed- 1s by-who 3m-love-you

      'I passed by the person who loves you'

   b. ?inna-kum qawmun ta-jhaluun

      verily –you people-a- ignore-pm

      'Verily, you are a people who are ignorant'

   c. <u>rajulun</u> jaa?a

      man-a came- 3sm

      'a man came'

     In (51a) the returning clitic ju- falls back on man 'who'. In (51b) the returning clitic -ta falls back on the pronoun –kum 'you-plu' and agrees with it in terms of person. In (51c) the clitic is contained in the verb and falls back on rajul 'man' and agrees with its number, person and gender (Wright, 1975, pp. 256, 319).

1.4.4.5. Two alternative answers to cliticization

     Summarizing, we first saw Kayne's ILM which predicted that any NSL (Null Subject Language) would allow clitic (long) movement. His claim is refuted by at least two strong NSL languages; namely Beber and

Arabic. We also saw Ouhallah's CPC which would be at best descriptively adequate to handle objective clitics in (some) Berber dialects. Finally, we saw how traditional Arab grammarians handled the clitics- all cases- but left, however, a few loopholes and discrepancies in their classification of the nominative clitics. The status of the subject fluctuated between cliticization and hidden (empty subject).

As a remedy to the above treatments, we will suggest a universal (clitic)-movement based on CPS (*), or alternatively a base-generation of clitic/agreement markers.

1.4.4.5.1. Clitic Placement Step (*) (CPS*):

Clitics will move/attach to their (local) governor, namely the V *daraba* 'hit' (52a) the *kitaab* 'book' (53b) or the *la* 'to' (52c):

(52) a. daraba-hu   Ali

    hit- 3sm-him Ali

    'Ali hit him'

b. kitaabu-hu

book-his

'his book'

c. la-hu

to-him

'to him'

The distribution of objective, genitive and oblique clitics is regulated by one-step CI-movement as shown (53):

(53) a. daraba-hu Ali t

b. Kitaabu-hu t

c. la- hu t

It may be argued that other languages, such as Italian and Beber, allow further steps while yet others allow now. To capture these generalizations and achieve a unified account of clitic movement, we suggest a step-by-step fashion formulated as follows:

(54)

CPS*: a clitic will move/incorporate in a step (*) fashion (UG). (where (*) stands for {0, 1, 2...x} times-language specific parameter).

So in English (*) stands for naught as in (55)

(55) John opened it with the key

In Arabic (*) equals one step as in (56):

(55) fataha-haa Ali t

opened-3sm-it Ali

'Ali opened it'

In Berber and Italian (*) equals two as in (56):

(56) a. ?a-t-irzam Ali ss-saruut

will-it-open 3sm Ali with-key

'Ali will open it with the key'

(Raouraou, p.c.)

b. Gianni le vuole leggere

Gianni them-want-3sm read-to

'Ginnani wants to read them'

Ouhalla's CPC/swoop fashion raises further problems in any attempt of generalization to coverV-movement as seen in (37) repeated here as (57):

(57)

a. AGR   TNS   V   CI

b. CI   V   AGR   TNS   t   t

c. * les oli-ont-r

The CPC/swoop fashion leads to aberrant output (57c).

Hopefully, the suggested CPS (*) could generalize further to apply to 'move alpha':

(58) Move Alpha (*): any item can move step (*)

In a language like Chinese which allows no syntactic movement (in question)

(*) will stand for naught (59a). In Arabic (relativization) it equals one step (59 b). In English (interrogatives) it equals many (59 c):

(59) a. Zhangsen wen wo shei mai-le shu

Zhangsen ask I who buy- ASP book

' Zhangsen asked me who bought books'

(aoun 1986, p.11)

b. ʔat-kitaabu llaəii fataḥu-hu

the-book that-sm open- 1st-it

'the book I opened'

c. who did you say   t   he saw   t

1.4.4.5.2. Agreement/clitics

Chomsky (1986, p. 13) emphasized specifier-head agreement, while traditional Arab grammarians focused on *ʔism-taabic* 'head-complement agreement. If we could collapse the two instances of agreement under 'head-modifier' agreement we may consider clitics as modifiers and at the same time agreement markers.

In the X-bar schemata the modifier (spec/comp) is the optional item, while the head is compulsory. This results in four options. (see Ben Rochd 1994a)

(60) [$_{x''}$ Mod [$_{x'}$ X [Mod]]]

This is illustrates in (61)

(61) [the old [boys [of the village]]]

In Arabic, the clitic/ agreement item would be a (post) modifier of a head such as N and would some argument X" outside its governing category (viz. NP, VP, PP, AP, IP, CP):

(62) X" i...[$_{NP}$ kitaabu (-hum$_i$ e$_i$)]

'their book'

1.4.4.6. Conclusion

In this section, I have tried to sketch a plausible universal grammar of cliticization. My goal was mainly to show that clitic movement and head-movement in general (move alpha, eventually) proceed in a step-by-step fashion (the number of steps being a language specific parameter).

It has been hopefully demonstrated that neither Kayne's ILM nor Ouhalla's CPC were adequate to handle Berber and /or Romance clitics, let alone be generalized to UG. Rather, we consider a step-by-step CPS (*) as pertaining to Universal Grammar. Or, the alternative would be to consider the clitic as a modifier (vs head) agreeing with an argument outside its governing category.

According to Popper, one cannot expect finality in any scientific investigation. Of many competing theories, we can at best determine which one is better. Concerning cliticization, I would therefore favour Clitic-Movement as it is more akin to the nature of Transformational Grammar.

NOTES

1. According to Radford (1981, p.63) the term 'pronoun' is doubly erroneous as it fails to describe the distribution as well as the coreference of words such as <u>him</u>, <u>her</u>, etc. He suggests rather to call them 'proforms'.

2. Clitic is defined as a form which resembles a word, but which cannot stand on its own, being dependent on a neighbouring word such as some pronouns in Italian and Spanish which attach to the end of a verb. (Crystal 1985, p.64)

3. Subjacency: Movement cannot cross more than one bounding node, where bounding nodes are IP and NP. (Haegeman 1991, p.41).

4. ECP is defined as follows: e must be properly governs B if A θ-governs or antecedent-governs B). The effects of the ECP can be seen in the following paradigm:

a. who do you think [t that [John saw e]]

b. who do you think [t [e left]]

c. who do you think [t that [e left]]

(Chomsky 1981, p. 260).

While Binding theory deals with A-binding, the ECP was devised to deal with A-bar binding. Aoun (1986) suggests to incorporate the two in his Generalized Binding theory:

5. HMC: Movement of an $X°$ category B is restricted to the position of a head. A governs maximal projection C of B where A theta-governs of L-Marks C. (Chomsky 1986, p.71 & Ouhalla 1989, p. 173).

6. AGR stands for "agreement", TNS stands for "tense" and INFL for "inflection".

Inflection is defined as a process of word formation. Inflectional affixes signal grammatical relationship, such as plural, past tense and possession, and do not change the grammatical category of the words to which they are attached; that is the word constitute a single paradigm, e.g., walk, walks, walked. A word is said to inflect for past tense, etc. (Crystal 1985, p. 184).

7. The definition of 'government' is fluctuating between Chomsky (1981) and Chomsky (1986) as in (a) and (b) respectively:

a. [c...A...B...]

In such configuration, A is an immediate constituent of C, A governs (c-commands) B. (Chomsky1981, p. 21).

(b) A governs B if A m-commands B and every barrier for B dominates A. (where barrier is X" which is not lexically marked) (Chomsly 1986, p.8)

8. The term 'MVC' is mine

9. Theoretically, Ouhalla's taxonomy hardly tallies with X-bar schemata; for VSO languages, he suggests the following tree:

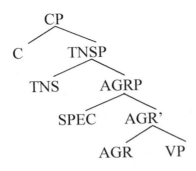

This configuration would fail to handle to handle sentences like: matta Rwaad li-ya-ʃkad (Berber, Tinoudi, p.c) who that will-3sm-come

A more orthodox tree would be as follows:

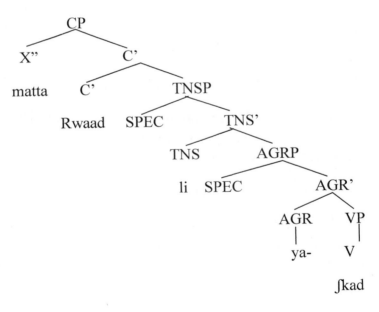

Also if AGR is too be considered the nominative case assigner of the subject then 'government' should be defined as in Chomsky (1986) viz; m-command rather than c-command.

10. The vowel /i/ is inserted as a consonant cluster breaker

a. t-tt   t-i-tt

b. CCC   CVCC

11. Enuniciative for traditional Arab grammarians is the equivalent of topicalization of TG grammarians.

12. Traditional Arab grammarians had a dependency approach based on government, which blurred their constituency outlook. They also confused ?ism 'noun' with 'noun phrase'.

13. Concerning the nominative pronoun, traditional Arab grammarians actually disagreed whether to consider it a clitic or an (empty) hidden pronoun plus an agreement.

APPENDIX

Base generation of clitics is assumed in Aoun (1986). Aoun established a table foe different types of anaphoric relations, depending on the position of their antecedent (see 1.4). He suggests that the clitic is in A-bar position and that the combination clitic-empty-category in an instance of (A-bar/A). This clitic is assumed to be in a A-bar position, whereas the empty category it blinds, is in an A position.

The clitic alone can be either a pronominal subject to generalized binding principle (B) as in (a) or an anaphor subject to generalized binding principle (A), as in (b)

(a) Jean$_i$ le$_j$ voit

(b) Jean$_i$ see$_i$ voit

1.5. Chomsky's Minimalist Program & Arabic Non-Concatenative Morphology

"How can a system such as human language arise in the mind/brain, or for that matter, in the organic world, in which one seems *not to find* systems with anything like the basic properties of human language?" (Chomsky)

INTRODUCTION

Ever since its earliest insemination in the fifties Chomsky's TRANSFORMATIONAL GRAMMAR has gone through consistent stages in its evolution; each time suggesting an elegant set of components for the description of natural language; e.g. phrase structures, lexicon and Transformations (Standard Theory). It stimulated many and moved into many different and sometimes contradictory directions. The advent of Chomsky's Minimalist Program in the nineties, was quite controversial. Many linguists wondered; it raised many questions in their minds: 'is it a theory of language? A philosophy about 'man's position in the organic world? An answer to the psychological problem of language learnability? or even an attempt to address the biological enigma of language? Is minimalist program a natural step in the evolution of Transformational grammar or rather a bewildering regression? In what sense does it differ from earlier versions of Transformational grammar; in its scope, principles or simply nomenclature?

Schools of linguistics and theories of language differ indeed. They confront and sometimes contradict each other. Linguists disagree amongst themselves. Language remains the same! This paper will be much narrower in scope. It will consider only Chomsky's Transformational grammar in its landmarks as can be found in major books such as *Aspects of The Theory of Syntax*,(1965) *Lectures on Government and Binding* (1981) and more particularly *The Minimalist Program* (1997). It will try to dishevel a few of its bewildering jargon, such as: 'procrastinate', 'attract/move', 'Chomsky's Greed', 'LCA' etc. (see their equivalent in the standard theory). (For introduction to TG grammar, see Andrew Radford's excellent book *Transformational Syntax* 1981)

1.5.1. PHILOSOPHY

The minimalist program is concerned with the place of language in the human mind/brain. So it is a cognitive theory of language. It tries to answer the psychological question: why is it possible for the child to learn language but not for any other biological creature? It even tries to answer the philosophical question about man's uniqueness in the organic world? Language seems to be unique among the cognitive systems, and man seems to be unique!

Sure enough, there are tensions and conflicts (as mentioned above). According to Chomsky, they concern the difference between observational, descriptive and explanatory theories of language; respectively those that state which sequences of sounds are (un)acceptable in a given language (1a), those which state that plus describe their structure (1b,c) and finally those which optimally provide explanatory principles for language acquisition (1d):

(1)

a. *sincerity may frighten the wall (vs. Sincerity may frighten the boy)

b. [s[NP The old man][PP in the corner]][VP is waiting [PP for the bus]]]

c. [s[NP The nasty woman][VP chased [NP the nice cat]]]

d. Minimalist Program/LCA

1.5.2. MINIMALIST GUIDELINES

(2)

- A linguistic expression is a pair (a, b) generated by the minimal derivation satisfying interface conditions

- The interface levels are the only levels of linguistic representation (PF/LF)

- All conditions concern the interface

- Derivations concerned are driven by morphological properties (attract/move)

- Economy is expressed in terms of greed and procrastinate (see below).

1.5.3. MINIMALIST MODEL:

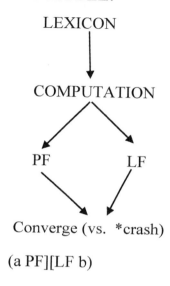

LEXICON

COMPUTATION

PF   LF

Converge (vs. *crash)

(a PF][LF b)

(3)

a. The ball was hit   t (English)

b. man jaa?a t   'who came'

c. John gave Mary a book t

d. sa-ja-qra?-u-haa   'he will read it'

e. ?al-baTTatu llatii ?akal-naa-haa 'the duck we ate'

(Ouhalla 004)

The new tree-diagram for sentence structure looks as follows:

(4)

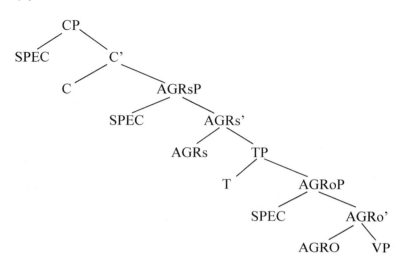

It considers all inflections as heads viz. Complementizers (C), tense (T), subject agreement(AGRs), object agreement (AGRo), as in sa-ja-qra?u-haa 'he will read it'.

(5)

a. [AGRs T AGR]

b. [AGRo V AGR]

(6)

a. [AGRs sa-ja]

   future-3m

b. [AGRo qra?u-haa]

   read-3sfACC

(7) Ahmed mudir 'Ahmed (is) director'

(8) ?acriD can hathaa .. 'Turn away from this' (The Quran 12:29)

(9)

Chomsky's Greed will presumably motivate all morpho-syntactic Transformations. (see below)

(10)

a. John will/-ed come

b. kitaabu Zaid-in   'Zaid's book'

c. Zaid kataba kitaab 'Zaid wrote a book'

1.5.4. LANGUAGE TYPOLOGY (SVO/VSO)

Considering the differences between SVO languages, like English and VSO languages like Irish, Chomsky (1997) assumes that, V raises overtly to I (AGRS) in Irish, while S and O raise in the LF component to SPEC AGRS and SPEC AGRO, respectively. We have only one way to express these differences: in terms of the strength of the inflectional features. One possibility is that the NP-features of TENSE is strong in English and weak in Irish; hence NP must raise to SPEC-IP in English prior to SPELL-OUT or the derivation will not converge; the procrastinate principle bars such raising in Irish. The EPP (extended projection principle), which requires that SPEC-IP be realized (perhaps an empty category), reduces to morphological property of tense: strong or weak NP-FEATURES features. Note that the NP-feature of AGR is weak in English, or we would have overt object-shift. We are still keeping to the minimal assumption that AGRS and AGRO are collections of features, with no relevant subject-object distinction, hence no difference in strength of features. Note also that a language might allow both weak and strong inflection, hence weak and strong NP-features: Arabic is a suggestive case, with SVO versus VSO correlating with the richness of visible verb-inflection. (Chomsky 1997)

In Irish the following phrase structures are noted:

(11)

a. Thainig Sean (Bob Quinn)

'came John'

b. Thaining (se)

'came he'

c. Feiceann Seán Mary.

'Sees John Mary'
d.   Chonac Seán Mary

'Saw John Mary'

e. Tá Seán mór.
'Is John big'
(Tall = árd/ Big = Mór)

From the above phrases, we notice that Irish is a VSO language, probably also a pro-drop, cop-drop language and a modifier last.

Arabic has the following sentence dichotomy:

(12) jaa?a l-?awlaad-u

Came-3m def-boys-NOM

(13) ?al-?awlaad-u jaa?-uu

The-boys came-3mp-NOM

(14) ?allah-a ?a-dcu

Allah-OBJ I call

(15) WEAK   STRONG   BOTH

SVO   SVO   WEAK   STRONG

VSO   SVO   VSO/SVO

IRISH   ENGLISH   ARABIC

1.5.5. TENSE OR ASPECT?

Ouhalla (1989) notes that in Semitic languages verbal roots consist of consonant clusters only, which are mapped onto vocalic melodies that constitute independent functional morphemes/categories.

(16) k-t-b

Zaid-un kataba kitaaban   'Zaid-NOM wrote a book-OBJ'

(17)

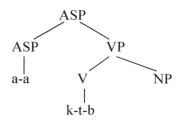

Arabic imposes a peculiar morphology. Each word consists of a root of three letters which express a general concept (Ben Rochd 1995) which is linked to an amazing network of sense relations such as gender, number, voice, aspect, etc. which are expressed by a set of melodies. These are actually linked to different valencies at the Logical Form when combined; the root and the melodies yield different words or assign different grammatical features to the same word as mentioned before.

1.5.6. NON-CONCATENATIVE MORPHOLOGY

As McCarthy (1979) put is there is no relationship between the form of the source and the form of the output in non-concatenative languages like Arabic. Rather, there is a blending of different syntactic and semantic information.

(18)

WRITING

k-t-b   **ROOT**

124

ø -uu   i-aa aa-i **MELODIES**

maktuub   kitaab kaatib

'Destiny' 'book'   'writer'

(19)* su-ʔil-at 'She was asked'

(20) qutilat 'She was killed'

(21) ya-kfii-ka-hum 'He suffices-you-them'

(22)

    u-i   PASSIVE

'to ask' s-ʔ-l –at FEMININE MARKER

1.5.7. PERFECTIVE TRANSFORMATION

(23)

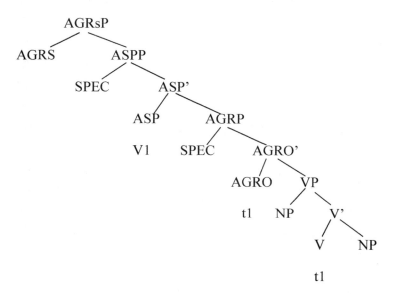

In Arabic, this morpho-syntactic operation consists of adding the prefix ja- (AGRs) to the perfective form so as to obtain the imperfective form:

(24)

a. Daraba ja-Dribu 'he hit'

b. Xaraja ja-Xruju 'he went out'

c. daXala ja-dXulu 'he came in'

1.5.8. CASE FILTER

Case and attract/move are interdependent. They are needed to render sentences grammatical.

(25)

    a.   *it seems Bill to be happy/ Bill seemed to be happy

    b.   Kitaabu Zaid-in 'Zaid's book'

(26) [V faire][VP boire] le cheval le/*il

1.5.9. 4/10 AGREEMENT

Arabic NPs will obey the so-called 4/10 ratio. Each head noun will pick up 4 features out of a set of 10, which include case, definiteness, number and gender, as follows:

(27) ?ar-rajulu l-kariim-u 'the-generous the-man'

a.

1.NOMINATIVE   1/3

2.ACCUSATIVE

3.OBLIQUE

b.

4. DEFINITE   1/2

5. INDEFINITE

c.

6. SINGULAR   1/3

7. DUAL

8. PLURAL

d.

9. MASCULINE   1/2

10. FEMININE

$$[1 + 1 + 1 + 1/3 + 2 + 3 + 3 = 4/10]$$

1.5.10. CHOMSKY'GREED

Chomsky (1981) states, 'passive morphology, once again, is not necessarily associated with movement and assumption of a new GF. Much the same still will be true in languages in which intransitives can be passivized as in Arabic, German, or Hebrew: sira yawa ljumu?ti.'

(28)

a. sira yawa ljumu?ati   (Arabic)

'travelled pass.on Friday'

    c.   es wurde getanzt   (German)

    d.   'it was danced'

    e.   dubar ba   (Hebrew)
    f.   'was spoken about her'

PASSIVE

(29)

Kataba   kutiba

CaCaCa NP1 NP2 → CuCiCa NP2

   Agent theme   theme

   NOM OBJ   NOM

ERGATIVE

(30)

?in-qataca l-Hablu

'The rope was broken'

CAUSATIVE

(31)

?acTaa Zaid-un camran kitaab-an 'Zaid gave Amr a book'

   CAUSER CAUSEE THEME

   NOM   OBJ OBJ

REFLEXIVE

(32)

Kaataba nii Zaid

Wrote+ref 1s-Zaid

NP1 CaCaCa NP2 → CaaCaCa NP1 NP2

           A/R A/R

(33)

    a.   falfala jufalfilu
       to put pepper (on the food)

    b. Sarufa jaSrufu

      to become noble

    c. calima jaclamu

      to know

    g.   daraba jadribu
       to hit

The perfective middle vowel transformation operates as follows:

(34)

    a. u → u

    b. i → a

    c. a → i

1.5.11. PHONETIC FORM IN ARABIC

Chomsky (1997), 'we expect languages to be very similar at the LF level, differing only as a reflex of properties at PF.' Arabic differs from other languages – say English by displaying the following (PF) syllabic patterns:

(35)

a. (C*) (V*)

b. #*CCC

c. #*VVVV

d. #*CC

e. #*V

f. #*CVCVCVCVCV

While LF is universal, each language tends to have its own PF principles. So in (35) we have some of the specific PF principles of Arabic. For example /split/ which consists of an initial cluster of three consonants is allowed in English but not in Arabic, neither a succession of four vowels as in /I eat/. The natural syllable structure is CV but condition (35f) seems to constrain it to three only.(Ben Rochd 1994a)

1.5.12. LOGICAL FORM

As stated above languages are supposed to be similar at LF. A natural economy condition would favour LF movement (transformations) as 'cheaper' than overt movements. Chomsky (1997) calls this principle 'procrastinate.'

(36)

a. whom$_1$ did John persuade t$_1$ [to visit t$_2$]

b. *whom$_2$ did John persuade whom$_1$ [to visit t$_2$]

No element can escape a position it could have reached by a shorter move, had that position not been filled. Ouhalla (1989) suggests the order of non-lexical categories in French as follows:

(37) a. [AGRP AGR [TNSP TNS [VP V]]

Ont   -er   arriv

(38)   *les ont-er-arriv

Ouhalla (1989) suggests his clitic one swoop movement condition (CPC) as an answer to Clitic-placement. He then tries to generalize it to head movement including V-movement, and finally moves to universal grammar. Applied to French his CPC/swoop leads to the aberrant output (38).

Arabic allows one step movement, while English allows one (or more). Chinese, which is said to have a procrastinate (no wh-movement), would have an LF movement of its operator-anaphors, leaving trace/variable itself controlled by the ECP.

(39)

a. Allah ?adc-uu   t 'God I pray'   (Arabic)

b. who did you say he saw? (English)

c. Zangsan wen wo [shei mai-le shu]   (Chinese)

ask I [who buy-ASP book]

1.5.13. LCA SUPERSEDES X-BAR

In the mid-nineteen's Kayne advanced his LCA (Linear Correspondence Axiom) to supersede all previous attempts (in syntax studies i.e. ICA, PSG, TG, X-bar) by suggesting the so-called notion of "asymmetric c-command," which can supposedly explain the surface word order of a sentence from its node structure, and ultimately work across language typology (SVO-VSO-OVS, etc.) to reach UG ultimately!

It can be formulated as follows: "the set of asymmetric c-command relations (of non-terminals) corresponds to the set of precedence relations (of terminals), as illustrated by the tree below:

133

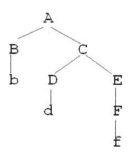

Putting aside the case of top-node A, node B asymmetrically c-commands D, E and F: [B>(D, E,F)], while D asymmetrically c-commands F only :[D > F]. Therefore the terminal string will be b-d-f. As an example from English, consider:

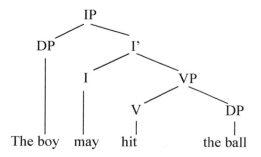

LCA aims at predicting surface word order from bare phrase structure. This would play down the dichotomy deep/surface structures, transformation (?) and predict very neatly the surface ordering of words in sentences across linguistically.

Applying LCA to Arabic possessive DPs, Kremers (2003) suggests:

134

(40)

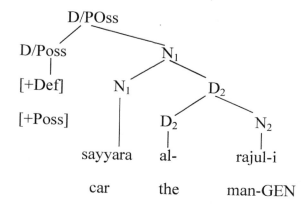

For Arabic VSO sentences Khalayli (1997) suggests:

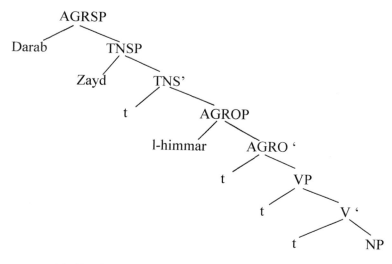

hit Zayd the Donkey

(From Khalaily, simplified)

Still, LCA does raise a few questions concerning what was called "flat-structure languages", government-case assignment, cop-drop, amongst a few features as is the case of Arabic syntax. Consider the sentences: *Walid Daraba l-Kura* 'Walid hit the ball,' *Daraba Walid l-kura* 'hit walid the ball' *and Walid sacid* 'Walid (is) happy.' The first sentence would pose no problem to LCA, as it is similar to English SVO order, the second one is a VSO and the third a so-called nominal sentence. For the second one, V would need some target head to attract/move to. For the last one, a so- called nominal sentence, we may suppose again the SVO with an empty copular (*yakuun* 'to be') in the verb slot.

CONCLUSION

Arabic has particular linguistic features:

a. It has a set of pharyngeals and velarized sounds. It requires initial glottal stop, as in the definite article /?al/ rather than /al/. It has a special PF (see above).

b. SVO, VSO, OSV word-orders are attested (sometimes optional) perhaps stylistically motivated, e.g. to say *?al-Xubza ?aakul* (OVS), means 'I will eat bread only', whereas if you say *?aakulu l-Xubz* (VSO), it means 'I will eat bread but I am ready to eat anything else.' None of these is ungrammatical, nor *greed* motivated?

c. Arabic has ASP rather than TNS.

d. All initial NPs are nominative.

e. Island Constraints hold.

f. Arabic Non-Concatenative Morphology.

For these features, Arabic may (or may not) challenge Kayne's LCA and/or Chomsky's Minimalist Program for that matter.

2. OCCAM's Razor[1]

TG theory has lately witnessed a prolifiration of heads and their equivalent projections: V/VP, N/NP, Adj/AdjP, P/PP, I/IP, C/CP, AGR/AGRP, TNS/TNSP, ASP/ASPP, Clitic/CIP(?), Q/QPn D/DP, a proliferation of principles: X-bar, government, ө, Case, Projection Principle, Extended Projection Principle, Empty Category Principle, and Case types: Structural Case, Inherent Case, Absolute Case, Exceptional Case, Absorbed Case. At LF (and S-structure) there are many anaphoric relations: A and A-bar anaphors, bound variables, anaphoric pronominals. In a spirit of 'economy of derivation' similar to the one suggested in Chomsky (1992), I will try and use Occam's razor to reduce, as much as possible, the above mentioned prolifiration of heads. The seven parameters will be reduced to two; namely X' and Move alpha (playing down Extended Projection Principle and ECP). Case types will be reduced to [α nominative]. And, finally A and A-bar anaphors (both full and empty) will be collapsed to one instance only: bound variable.

2.1. Parametric theory

The aim of TG theory is to give unified accounts for different and seemingly unrelated linguistic phenomena. This UG compromises parameters and principles. Chomsky (1982) suggested a system of principles as an alternative to the previous system of rules (see 1.4)[2]

Besides these major principles, TG assumes minor principles such as the Projection Principle (which we deduce from head complementation), the Extended

Projection Principle (which are from Head specification) and the Empty Category Principle which may be seen as part of Bounding theory, and which may prove obsolete in languages using cliticization (see below).

2.1.1. X- bar Theory

X-bar theory holds primarily at d-structure yielding a set of configurations which are mapped onto s-structure thanks to the COMPUTING SYSTEM as in (1):

(1) **d-s** -----> COMPUTUNG (X-bar, move alpha) -----> **s-s**

The notion "head" plays a crucial role in X-bar theory (as well as in the best of this model). It consists of grammatical functions (GF) such as "subject", "object", "complement", etc. It enters into the assignment of θ-roles in sentences and phrases. Consider the following sentences:

(2) They killed John (Chomsky, 1981)

(3) John was killed t

(4) John's pictures of Bill

In (2), we know that <u>John</u> is the object of the head verb <u>kill</u>, which assigns the theta role "theme" (alas victim) to it. This θ-assignment takes place at d-structure. This is true also in (3), although <u>John</u> appears in a different position. Its (original) argument position is marked by t which indeed receives the theta role theme, being the

142

object of the verb <u>kill</u>. In (4) John is "agent" while Bill may be seen as "benefactive". (Lyons 1977)

The properties of d-structure – such as θ-roles follow from the Projection Principle, which states that every θ-role is assigned at d-structure by a head uniquely, to some argument NP and is preserved throughout the derivation at s-structure and LF.

Chomsky (1986b) assumes a sophisticated system for X-bar (see 1.4.3). The conventional symbols NP, VP, AP, PP are alternatively replaced by N", V", A", P" (for the maximal projections of the lexical categories: N, V, A and P). the complementation options are quite limited. And in the case of transitive verbs, the maximum is three in Arabic (Ali, p.c):

(5)

?Xbar-tu-hu I-Xabara haqqan

told-I-him   the-news truth

The verb ?Xbartu 'informed' seems to hold three complement NPs –hu 'him   I-Xbara 'the news' and haqqan 'the truth'.

Chomsky (1986b) suggests an extension of X-bar schemata to cover functional categories such as Inflection (I) and complementizer (C). This would turn the traditional, clausal categories S and S' into IP and CP, respectively, as in (6):

(6)

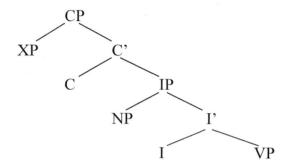

Chomsky (1986a) ignored a further distinction that can be drawn between two types of postnominal phrases – viz, complements and adjuncts. One possible way of telling which is which through nominalization in which ө-roles resurface more clearly. Consider (7):

(7):

a. The King of England

b. The king with six wives

c. The king of England with six wives

Radford (1988) summarizes the above structures as in (8)

(8)

a. Determiners expand N-bar into N-doublebar

b. Adjuncts expand N-bar into N-bar

c. Complements expand N into N-bar

(9)

[N" The [N'[N' king of England] [PP with six wives]]]

     Phrase structure rules can now be dispensed with entirely. We assume that X-bar structuring is responsible for government, theta marking and ultimately case (after move alpha has applied). The nominal, however, seem to have posed a problem (cf. Chomsky 1986b, Abney 1986, Stowell 1989 and Fassi Fahri 1990). Consider (10):

(10)

(the) pictures of John

In (10) <u>pictures</u> functions as the head noun. It is expanded into N' thanks to the prepositional phrase <u>of John</u>, and <u>the</u> in turn expands N' into N". Chomsky claims that N is the head of the noun phrase and that N' can be dispensed with when there is no determiner as in <u>pictures of John</u>. Stowell (1989), Abney (1986) and others have chosen D instead of N as head.

Stowell (1989) deals with two related questions: the relationship between the subject position and the specifier position in terms of X-bar theory, and the relationship between the determiner and the noun in what he calls Common Noun Phrase (CNP in neutral terms). The crucial point is centered around the choice of the head of the CNP: is it N or D? (see below)

In Ouhalla (1988), we witness another type of proliferation of functional heads which are linked to V-movement. This is postulated so as to account for (VSO) Sentential Structure. His purpose is to reanalyze the structure of sentential clauses Romance and (Hamito) semitic languages. The main argument is that the inflectional elements A GR, TNS and NEG belong under the I-node (see Ben Rochd 1994a).

Chomsky (1981) suggests a sort of link between different levels of derivation s-s, d-s and LF; called Projection Principle which assures that verbs for instance θ-mark their complements (as heads do) as can be seen in passives or nominals:

(11)

a. The city was destroyed.

b. The city's destruction

The subject position is not θ-marked like the complements as can be seen in (12):

(12)

a. John was killed

b. John's refusal of the offer

The subject position is not θ-marked by V (Chomsky calls this indirect θ-marking by VP).

We also notice that non-arguments such as pleonastic dummies (cf. Bennis 1990) can occupy the subject position:

(13)

Il pleut

There are also languages that allow a "null subject" such as Romance languages and Semitic languages

(14)

a. e parla

(he) spoke

b. jaa?a

(he) came

c. * saw Mary

The projection Principle and the requirement that clauses have subject (14) are quite closely related (cf. headship). So Chomsky (1982) sees that the two principles are reducible to one general principle he refers to as the Extended Projection Principle. We consider the latter as deducible from Head- complement and Head- specifier, in terms of X-bar (Chomsky 1986b).

Among the various types of relations holding between syntactic elements such as heads and complement phrases, three appear to be crucial in determining barrierhood: (i) the relation between a head and the complement phrases to which it assigns Case ө-role (or both ideally), (ii) agreement such as the one between a head and a specifier and (iii) the coindexing relation known as "chain". The first relation is referred to as "head marking" and the last as CHAIN COINDEXING. "When a head happens to be lexical such as N, V, P or Adj head marking is referred to as LEXICAL MARKING. The latter relation holds particularly when defining barrierhood. A barrier is a non- L-marked maximal projection, as in (15)

(15)

a.?acrifu Zaid-an

I know Zaid-obj

b. …that [IP…]

c. ?acrifu ?anna[IP zaid-an…]

I know that   Zaid-obj

In (15b) the matrix verb ?acrifu assigns objective case to Zaid; being its object. In (15c) IP is not L-marked (by the complementizer ?anna) therefore it functions as a barrier for the government of the matrix verb.

L-marking enters also, crucially in the definition of proper government (i.e., ECP). A trace will be properly governed (at s-structure or LF) if it is L-marked by N, V, P or Adj:

(16)

a. who did you say that he saw t

b. * who did you say that t saw him

The crucial difference between (16a) and (16b) is that the trace t in the first sentence is L-marked by the verb see, while in the second it is not (that being functional).

Θ marking has to meet the conditions of "sisterhood" which is expressible in terms of X-bar theory not independently of government (as assumed in Chomsky's 1986 b). A head A will θ-marks only if B is the complement of A in the sense of X-bar theory (m-command holding). It is also assumed here that the specifier is also head marked (m-commanded). Note that "sisterhood" is defined here in terms of head-marking which makes both complement and specifier subject to head government (case-government, see below).

2.1.2. Move Alpha (Bounding theory)

It is assumed that there are two types of movement: substitution and adjunction. The former has certain constraints. (see section 4)

(17) * Where [IP in the middle of t]] No item can cross more than one bounding node in a swoop fashion (where bounding node is taken to be a maximal projection X")

Chomsky (1986b) discusses the (exceptional) case government of the subject of SMALL CLAUSES from the matrix clause, and their connection to the filter (on Move Alpha).

(18) They consider [John] AP intelligent]

Notice that <u>consider</u> does not θ-mark the subject of the small clauses, <u>John</u> in (18). Nevertheless, the subject of a small clause can be extracted from wh-island as in (19) (as it satisfies ECP):

(19)

Who did they want to consider [t [to be] intelligent]

The same problem arises with Exceptional Case-marking constructions. Consider (20)

(20)

* John seems that [he considered [t [to be] intelligent]]

(20) is assumed to be an ECP violation. The trace t has no internal governor. The (abstract) Inflection (I) is not a lexical item. Notice, here, crucially, that the (adjectival) passive participle considered is not an L-marker either (cf. Ben Rochd 1982). But in (19) we are bound to conclude that t is in fact externally governed by the matrix verb <u>consider</u>.

One obvious difference between the two constructions lies in Case assignment: in (19) consider: assigns Case to the trace t (under government) but in (20) t does not receive Case. Chomsky assumes that in this case, it is "absorbed by passive". There is however an alternative option that assumes successive cyclic movement to VP, then to the matrix CP. This would yield the structure below:

(21) [VP t' [VP consider [t...]]]

2.1.3. Case theory

Chomsky (1981) sets the principles of Case theory; one of which is inherent case (see section 1.4.). Developing Chomsky's dichotomy INHERENT/STRUCTURAL CASES, Haegeman (1991) suggests the Structural Case assignment depends solely on government (and it is a configurational property) while Inherent Case depends on both theta role and government. Consider (22):

(22)

a. ?actaqidu (?anna) zayd-an faXuurun

believe – I (that) Zaid- obj   proud

b. ?ictiqaadi (?anna) zayd –an faXuuran

believe – my (that) Zaid – obj. proud

c. Ali faXuurun bi farasihi

Ali proud of horse- his

d.* Ali faXuurun farasi-hi

Ali proud horse-obl-his

Inherent case is defined as in (23):

(23)

A is an inherent case assigner for an NP assigns case and theta role to an NP.

We notice once again that adjectives as in (21b) are unable to case-govern and θ-mark their complements.

There is a further complication genitive case. In Chomsky (1986a) nouns (like ditransitive verbs) are assumed to assign genitive case inherently rather than structurally. It is further assumed that in English inherent genitive is realized by means of a preposition. There is thus an asymmetry between the abstract genitive case assigned inherently by the noun, and the concrete prepositional genitive case (cf. Haegeman 1991).

Inherent case condition (23) entails that nouns such as ?iciqaadii and adjectives such as faXuur will assign inherent genitive case to NPs which they theta-mark. So in (22c) for instance the NP faras will be assigned inherent case. So, inherent case goes hand in hand with theta-marking in contrast to structural properties of head government.

2.1.4. Binding Theory

Chomsky (1981-1992) set the principles of Binding theory that partitions nominal into three types: anaphors, pronominals and r-expressions; to deal with noun the reference properties of phrases (from complex NPs to ECd, not to forget clitics):

(24)

a. [NP The old man (who is) in the corner]

b. Les enfants [NP s'] amusent

c. [NP PRO] to feed each other ice-cream

(see Logical Form)

2.1.5. Control Theory

Control theory is the module of the grammar concerned with assignment of reference to null subjects in infinitive and gerundive complement and adjunct clauses:

(25)

a. John tried [PRO to leave]

b. John considered [the PRO leaving]

(Stowell 1989, Borer 1991)

c. [wa huwa jaqtacu ttariiqaa] Zaid ra?aa marjama

    and he crossing the street   Zaid saw Mary

d. [kawnu-hui yanjahu fi l- ?imtihaan] yufrihu zajdi

    be-he   he-succeed in exams it -please Zaid

Arabic hardly allows ungoverned anaphoric pronominal PRO (see below). In (25b) the agent argument would be again a post nominal oblique pronoun. In (25c) PRO is simply impossible; the overt nominative pronoun huwa is obligatory. And likewise in (25d) a cliticized normative pronoun shows up. Coreference relations, however, still hold between those (clitic) pronouns and their antecedents, and hence the need for (co) indexing.

2.2. Occam's Razor

In this section, we will consider case-government (CG, henceforth) as crucial criterion for headship. This will help in reducing the heads N, D and Q (with their respective phrases N (and NP) only. DP will be rejected for the failure of its head to case govern its NP specifier, and the failure of the PRO distribution suggested in Stowell (1989).

Syntactically, it is obvious that Q has the distribution of N and so we will consider it to be. Demonstratives will be considered as full-fledged NPs because of their distribution (in typical GF positions). Genitive will be straightforward in our analysis; it is assigned by a governing N (m-commander) rather than pseud-of (Chomsky 1986a), traditional Arab grammarians annexation [N+N] or Chomsky's (1981) N' (inherent) government.

2.2.1. DP Hypothesis

Stowell (1989) deals with two related issues: the relationship between the subject position and the specifier in terms of X-bar theory, and the relationship between the determiner and N in what he calls Common Noun Phrase (CNP), in neutral terms. He raises the problem of the choice of the head of CNP: is it N or D? (as seen above).

He notes that there is a clear difference between adjectives and nouns in English (at least). Adjectives are predicates with their specific internal argument structure (ɵ-grid); whereas nouns may function as predicates or as referring expressions.

(26)

a. Zaid sahlu I-jaanibi (idiom)

'Zaid is easy to live with'

Another difference between nouns and adjectives is that the former but not the latter needs a determiner (in English, at least):

(27)

a. John is a daft

b. John is (quite) daft

(28)

a. the man read one book

b. * man read book

There is a further (and crucial) question which concerns the position of the determiner. There are different options suggested in Chomsky (1986b), Jackendoff (1977) and Abney (1986), (29a), (29b) and (29c) respectively:

(29)

a.

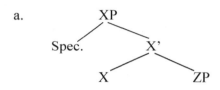

b.

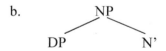

c.

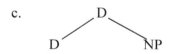

Notice that the spec-note in (29a) is not specified. The aim of Stowell (1989) is to review Chomsky's (1986b) X-bar principle B) so as to make it more consistent by expending it across syntactic categories so as to achieve a perfect symmetry between C, I and D:

(30)

B. X" = X" * X'

Stowell (1989) defends his generalization by postulating a subject (specifier) hypothesis as follows:

(31)

Every XP must contain a specifier position

He then tries to defend the DP hypothesis by noting that the distribution of PRO is crucial in this respect. PRO occurs in subject of infinitival IPs in so called control structures (the subject position of which is ungoverned). It also occurs in NP structures as in (32):

(32)

Bill resented [NP the PRO destruction of the city [IP PRO to prove a point]

The second issue concerns the head of the CNP; ie, are nominal better handled as NPs or DPs? In other words are they headed by N or D? Stowell refers to Jachkendoff's (1977) and Abney's (1986) approaches respectively (33a) and (33b):

(33)

a. [NP   DP   N']

b. [DP   D   NP]

(34)

a. [NP   the pictures]

b. [DP   the pictures]

Stowell defends Abney's hypothesis rather than Jachendoff's. His arguments are as follows: first, NPs are consistently used as predicates of Small Clauses (SCs), second, nouns (mass nouns, bare plurals, generic nouns and adjectives) are consistently predicative whereas Determiners are consistently referential:

(35)

a. Zajdun   rajulun

Zaid man-a

b. jaa?a haaɘaa

come   that

Third, PRO occurs in IPs and Small clauses. Stowell fails, however, to illustrate its distribution in CP and faces also wh-extraction which is (sometimes) blocked, in spite of the vacant DP specifier which is assumed to be a scape-hatch for wh-extraction:

(36)

a. I consider [John fascinating]

b. * I consider [PRO fascinating]

c. * who did Bill shoot [DP [NP t 's father]]

Note that (Arabic) quantification and demonstratives seem to pose a problem of double specification.

Consider (37):

(37)

a. əaaka   I-walad

   Det   Det

   *that   the boy

b. Kullu   I-?awlaadi

   all   the-   boys

c. tout les enfants

The first hypothesis of Stowell's is self-refuted as it does not specify the kind of specifier needed for NP/DP (X" or X° ?) The second argument based on the distribution of PRO is even less appealing as Stowell fails to show PRO's distribution in CP. There is also an obvious c-government of the PRO position in this own example:

a. They took advantage of us

b. Advantage was taken of us

c. We were taken advantage of

d. * The PRO taking of advantage...

When we substitute an overt NP for PRO, (genitive) case does show up, and consequently, we have to admit that that position is c-governed and therefore PRO cannot fix in. Borer (1989) has similarly refuted the very existence of PRO (so-called ungoverned empty category) reducing it to pro (see below).

Fassi Fehri (1990) also relies on Abney's (1986) DP hypothesis and tries to make the parallel between nominals and clausal IP structures in Arabic. He gives examples of NPs that are headed by a 'normal' N a that assigns no government to them (see below):

(39)

a. daXaltu   d-daar

   enter- I the- house

b. daXal-tu daara   ?al-rajuli

   enter- I   house   the-man

He considers also (complex) genitive and/ or gerundive constructions as in (40):

(40)

a. ? aqlaqani i darbu r-rajuli I-walada

   it- annoyed - me hitting the - man the - boy

b. ?aqlaqani   i darbu   rèrazjli li I-waladi

   it- annoyed   -me hitting the man-to the -boy

160

The problem is twofold: first, is S the projection of ASP, TNS, and AGR? If we choose the last option we would then be able to parallel NP with S? Fassi Fehri suggests that NP is the projection of Det (or alternatively AGR/clitic in derived nominals). We turn now to his DP hypothesis:

Det co-occurs with N and the latter carries the features number, gender and diminutive as shown in (41):

(41)

	N	?al
number	-un
gender	N
diminutive	ADJ

we can note further that there is a complemntary distribution between Det and annexed NP (NX):

(42)

?al- N   /   N -un

da ə aa /   N   NP

Following Abney (1986), Fassi Fehri assumes that the head of NP (sic) is Det rather than N as in (43):

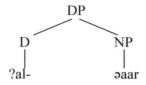

Det is considered as specifier of NP because of the complementary distribution between articles and an annexed NPs (see above). Det and annexed NP (?) can function as noun subjects, but the specifier can be filled by one or the other, but not both at the same time:

(44)

a. ə-əaar

the - house

b. ə-əaaru zajdin

house Zaid

c. *ə-əaaru zajdin

the- house Zaid

Fassi Fehri then moves on the to defend the second option, which shows a clear symmetry between nominals and S when they are both considered as projections of AGR:

(45)

```
              AGRP
           ╱       ╲
        AGR         DP
                  ╱    ╲
              SPEC      D'
                      ╱    ╲
                    D        NP
                           ╱    ╲
                       SPEC      N'
                         │        │
                       rajul    əaar (idiom)
```

The notion HEAD in our approach is based case-government (CG). And Case in turn is considered as the effect of Head government.

2.2.2. Headship

In Chomsky (1981) the notion 'head' seems quite confusing as it fluctuates between four heads: N, V, Adj and P which are expanded thanks to complement arguments (A-positions) into X" (Chomsky 1981: 47) and three heads 'The lexical categories are (+N, -V) ie. noun, (-N, +V) ie. Verb and (+N, +V) ie. Adjective" (Chomsky 1981: 48). Notice here that (-N, -V) ie. Preposition is excluded.

AGR has an even worse fate. It is once considered as a (head?) governor of empty categories in pro-drop languages (Chomsky 1981:250), and on another occasion it is explicitly specified, for the requirement of the ECP, that an empty category is properly governed if its governor is different from AGR. AGR is further assumed to assign nominative case to the subject of tensed clauses as in:

(46)

a. zajǝ-un juǝunnu [?anna-hu] ǝakij

b. John is considered [t   foolish] (Chomsky 1981)

In Chomsky (1986b) the things seem much more tidy concerning 'headship'. X-bar theory is based on the lexical notion 'head' which can be further split into a binary system of features [ὰ N, ὰV] yielding the categories; noun, verb, adjective and pre/postposition. Each head $X°$ has its specific projections X' and X'' (see above):

(47)

a. jaa?a   NP

came

b.?akal   NP   NP

ate

c. ?actaa NP   NP   NP

gave

d. ?aXbara   NP NP NP   (Ali, p.c.)

inform

e. ǝanna   NP   CP

think

In (47a) the lexical head jaa?a projects thanks to its specifier NP subject. In (47b) the lexical head ?akala projects to V' thanks to its complement NP and to V" thanks to its specifier NP subject. In (47c) ?actaa needs two complements NPs to project into V' and a specifier NP to yield V". In (47d) ?aXbara needs three complements (which is the maximum number allowed in Arabic). In (47e) əanna needs a CP complement and an NP subject.

GOVERNMENT is defined in Chomsky (1986b) as in (48):

(48)

A governs B if A m- commands B and there is no C, such that C a barrier for B and C excludes A.

This definition encompasses substitution as well as adjunction structures. It uses notions such as M-COMMAND, BARRIER and EXCLUDE.

The notion "m-command" can be defined as sisterhood (aunthood) under a common maximal projection X" (mother). In (49) man 'who' m – commands t – being both dominated by the maximal projection CP:

(49) $[_{CP}$ man $[_{IP}$ t $[_{I'}$ $[_{VP}$ ra?aa-hu]]]]

who   saw-him

165

Consider the paradigm below:

(51) They consider him intelligent

(52) They want an intelligent boy

(53) zadjdun   jaəannu   [camrun]

(54) NP   think   NP

    Zaid   3sm-thinks   Amar

(55) Zaid V [NP]

The NP in (54) takes eventually the status of the object of the matrix V as far as c-government and extraction are concerned.

It behaves like an object, and it is therefore c-governed by the matrix (although not ө-marked by it). C-government is straight forward and naturally defined in terms of X-bar.

The notion BARRIER itself could be challenged on these grounds (i.e., c-government). Maximal projections such as NP, IP and CP (Unless C is filled by its proper head cease to be barriers as they can be transparent to C-government by external heads, such as the matrix verb in complex sentences).

(55)

a. ra?ajtu [NP l-walada-a   t-tawii-la]

saw-I   the boy – OBJ   the-tall-OBJ

b. I made [the dog walks]

c. ?acrifu [CP   ?anna Zaid-an]

know-I   that Zaid-OBJ

DP is laso a defective maximal projection (if not a redundant one) as it permits external c-government of its own grounds (see above).

We will use the notion 'government – more specifically CASE-GOVERNMENT as the criterion for headship. A head will be a case governor. Head-Marking is considered as responsible for assigning Case (and/or ө-role) to complements. Consider (56):

(56)

a. suwwaru [NP1 – walad-i]

   pictures the-boy-gen

b. zaid-un   qara?a l-kitaab-a

   Zaid-NOM   read the-book-OBJ

c. zaid-un   yuriidu   [?islaaha s-saiiarat-i]

   Zaid- NOM   3-s- want to the repairing the –car

d. *(hijja) kaanat muhaddamatun l-madiinatu

   it was destroyed the city

e. faouqa [NP l-maa?idat-i]

on the-table-OBL

f. ?inna-hu qaa?im-un

that-he- OBJ   standing

g. zaid-un   kaana   qaa?im-an

Zaid- NOM was standing-OBJ

From (56) above, we can deduce that the lexical vs non-lexical dichotomy as established in Chomsky (1986b) requires some revision so as to cope with Arabic. Adjective should be eliminated from the lexical set. The reason for this is that it does not licence the full NP I –madi:nati 'the city' in (56d). It is actually the reason behind passive NP proposing in the first place.

We suggest to consider case- governors as "heads" (adjectives-excluding). The headship of AGR will be superseded by that of I. We also suggest the elimination of exotic case assignment such as the one concerning genitive and inherent case and dative. These will be replaced by N-government (CG) and P-government (CG) respectively. Consider (57):

(57)

a. ?al-rajulu   s-saalihu

the-man- nom   the- good-man

b. sajjaratu muhammad- in

168

car (of) Muhammad-gen

c. I gave a book to Bill

In (57b) muhammadin is assigned genitive case by being governed (m-commanded) by <u>sajjartu</u> rather than by POSS (abstraclty) or N' (oddly) as in Chomsky (1980) and (1981).

Consider (58):

(58)   [NP [N sajjavato] [NP muhammadin]]

There is another option, explored in the literature, which claims that there is a preposition which "is not a genuine preposition" (Ouhalla 1988) but rather a genitive case-marker. This would suggest the following d-structure for the above

(59)

[NP [N] [PP P NP]]

This option could be used to eliminate (exotic) inherent case by suggesting the same solution for dative –namely preposition- government (CG). Consider (60):

(60)

John gave a book to Bill

Bill is now assigned case by the preposition before PP preposing takes place (see below):

(61)

a. John gave a book to Bill

b. John gave Bill a book t

There is c-government of <u>a book </u>by <u>gave</u> and c-government of <u>Bill</u> by <u>to</u>. While in (61a) in (61b), there is PP-movement; known as DATIVE (not structure preserving).

Case could further be simplified by keeping only two outputs: [+ Nominative] and [- Nominative]. The latter would collapse objective, oblique, genitive, and dative. Consider the following data from Arabic:

(62)

a. safaha zaid – an / – hu

shook – he (hands with) Zaid –obj/- him

b. li/la zaid - in /- hu

to Zaid - obl/ him

c. kita: bu zaid - in/ - hu

book Zaid -gen /his

The clitic is a good diagnosis for c-government. We notice that objective, oblique and genitive clitics are one and the same, namely –hu (cf. Fassi Fehri (1989)).

2.3. Case

Al-Shorafat (1991) reviews case-government proposed in Chomsky (1981) and (1986b). The latter suggests that "if the category A assigns a case, then it may assign it to an element that it governs" also A and its governore must be adjacent. Consider (63):

(63)

a. I put the book on the table

b. * on the table the book I put

There is further a distinction between inherent case (as seen above) assigned by P and N (oblique and genitive) and structural case assigned at s-structure under government by I and V (nominative and objective):

(64)

a. kitaabu Zaid-in/li Zaid-in

book Zaid- GEN / to Zaid-OBL

b. kaana zajd - un jadribu camr -an

was Zaif – nom hitting Amr- obj

c. kataba zajd - un risaalat-a / Sukr- in li saahibi- hi

wrote Zaid – nom letter – obj thanking – gen to friend –obl- his-gen

Al-Shorfat notes the inadequacy of case as found in Chomsky (1981) and (1986) to handle the Arabic data.

Furthermore Arabic being a flat languages (Chomsky 1986a) both Infl and V c-command NP1 (subject) and

NP2 (object) and render the explanation of case unclear. Add to this that adjacency is not always satisfied.

Government explains case (in English at least) since case filter (65) would reject overt NPs such as <u>John</u> when found in ungoverned positions as subject of an infinitival:

(65)

* NP without case

(66)

a. *seems John to be sick

b. John seems   t   to be sick

John is forced to move to the initial position where it receives government-case. This does not seem to be the case in Arabic in which, case is assigned at d-structure and is preserved throughout:

(67)

a. ?akala zaydun ruzan

   ate Zaid rice- obj

b. ruzan   ?akala zajdun

   rice- OBJ   ate Zaid

c. ?akala ruuza-an Zaid-un

   at-e rice-OBJ Zaid-NOM

Al-Shorafat (1991) further presents minor categories such as particles and complemntizers as capable of case-governing just as major lexical categories are (cf. Chomsky (1981) and (1986b).

(68)

a. kaana I-jaww u baarid- an

was the – weather - nom cold -obj

b. ?nna I-jaww – a baarid- un

that the – weather – obj. cold- nom.

In an approach based on c-government by an m-commanding head, in terms of X-bar, the problems in Al-Shorafat (1991) simply evaporate. Consider (69):

(69)

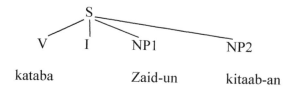

Al-Shorafat (1991) notes the confusion of government in such a tree, and in terms of c-command. He wonders which is which, ie which NP does V govern and which NP does INFL govern. In terms bar and m-command we suggest (70):

(70)

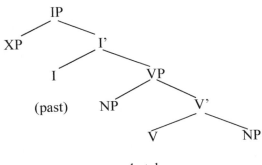

kataba

2.4. Noun Phrase or Small Clause?[5]

Dealing with Arabic, Fassi Fehri (1985) suggests the X-bar representation (71):

(71)

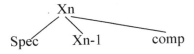

He then assumes that Arabic is a head – first language. Supposedly a noun phrase would begin with a noun, a prepositional phrase would begin with a preposition, a sentence would begin with a verb, and so on and so forth...

(72)

a. [NP [N kitaab]..]

b. [PP [P fawqa]]

c. [V" [V ?adcuu] [NP e] [NP Allah]]

174

call (I) Allah (Fassi-Fehri 1985)

Fassi Fehri's (1985) and (1990) X-bar branchings goes against the main stream of most generative grammarians, who have adopted the binary branching framework as in (73):

(73)
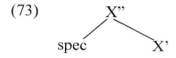

There is another area of confusion concerning (Arabic) nominals. Chomsky (1986a) assumes that typical Small Clauses (SCs) have a structure of the form:

(74) They consider [XP John [AP intelligent]]

Here XP is a projection of <u>intelligent</u> (so it is some sort of Adjectival phrase). Its specifier is <u>John</u>. It receives its θ-role from the head <u>intelligent</u>.

The solution we suggest, to clear away the confusion between noun phrases (NPs) and small clauses (SCs) respectively is to postulate the following diagram (75) for both constructions- the criterion being definiteness:

(75)

a. [ὰ Def]   [a Def]

b. [a Def]   [- Def]

Both NPs and SCs consist of two nominals constructs NC1 and NC2. The crucial difference between them is that the second nominal construct (NC2) of an SC is always indefinite while in an NP the two nominal constructs must agree in (in) definiteness. An NP will have feature [à Def] shared between its nominal constructs (NC1 and NC2).

2.5. QP hypothesis (and demonstratives)

Another redundancy affecting nominals structures is the QP phrase usually attached to the right (or left) of NPs. Consider the following configuration from Benmamoun (1993):

(76) a.

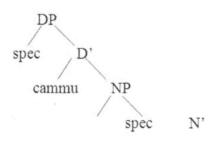

l- ?awalaad-i

'the-boys-GEN'

b.

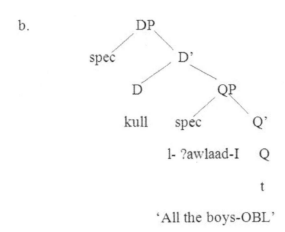

'All the boys-OBL'

Bennamoun considers cammu+NP and kullu+ QP as construct states (CSs) following Aoun (1978) and others). The head noun carriers the case assigned to the whole projection NP (?) and in turn assigns genitive case to the NP following it. In (76a) cammu carriers the nominative case of the whole DP and in turn assigns genitive case to its complement NP. Similarly kullu carriers the normative case of the whole DP and assigns genitive case to its complement QP.

In both cases Bennamoun assumes Head –to- Head movement (?), but fails to determine the nature of the specifier of NP, QP or even DP (this, recall was done to justify Stowell's Specifier hypothesis, alias, Chomsky's X-bar principle (B)).

We assume a much simpler option which consists of considering Q as a c-governing noun (77a), its projection an NP as it has the distribution of NPs (77b), and eliminating DP for the above stated reasors.

(77)

a. kullu n-aas-i

all the people- GEN

b. jaa?a l-kull-u/l-walad-u/ əaalika

came the all-NOM/ the-boy- NOM/ that- NOM

QPs and DPs have the GF of NPs and will be considered so. QPs and DPs have the GF of NPs and will be considered so.

2.6. Bound Variables

Anaphors are reflexives, traces, PRO^s. They can be considered as BOUND VARIABLES.

(78)

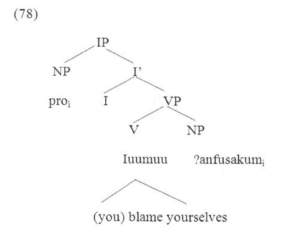

In Chomsky (1981) a governing category (NP or S) is postulated as a domain for (co)indexing (see above). Binding principle (B) is concerned with overt pronominals, essentially. The latter are necessarily case marked and hence assigned to a governing category in which they have a disjoint reference:

(79)

a. daXala Zaidun   [maktaba- hu]

   entered Zaid   office - his

b. jaəunnu Zaid   [CP ? anna – hu ə kiij]

   thinks Zaid   that - he clever

c. * jatawaqqacu Zaid ?an [pro jara: hu camr]

   excepted Zaid   see- him Amr

In each case the clitic –hu cannot be coindexed in its governing category (NP, S,…). A substitution of nafsihi 'himself' for the clitic would not work either.

Chomsky (1982) suggests his feature based approach to deal with the semantic properties (ANAPHORIC/PRONOMINAL) of empty categories (ECs):

(80)

a. Who [did you see t]

b. Advantage was taken t

(81)

a. pro jaa?a (Arabic)

(he) came

b. PRO to feed each other ice cream

The ECs in (80a) and (81) are A-bar bound variables, while the others are A-anaphors. Using standard logic, Aoun (1986) tries to collapse A and A-bar anaphors. The two can be assimilated to one instance of bound variable. This move does indeed embody a strong empirical claim: it unifies two classes of elements which exhibit similar properties. Consider (82):

(82)

a. Who loves his mother

b. His mother loves everyone

In (82a) the clitic pronoun his can be bound (in one reading) by who but cannot be bound (except in inclusion, perhaps) by the quantifier everyone in (82b).

NOTES

1. William of Occam: English nominalist philosopher who stood against the Pope in the 14c. He defended that entities should not be multiplied beyond necessity.

2. Thanks to X-bar theory, lexical categories can be limited to the minimum and phrase structure rules can be dispensed with entirely (Chomsky 1986b) vs (Fassi Fehri (1990,p. 48):

a. I" - - D"   I'

b. D"   D"   D'

c. I'   I   V"

3. For binding theory, the mother should be taken to be any branching node otherwise NPs a) and b) would violate Binding conditions:

a.

```
        N"
       /  \
     NP     ?
   The city  ┌──────────┐
             │          │
             └──────────┘
             deconstruction  t
```

b.

```
        N"
       /  \
     NP     ?
    Its    ┌──────────┐
           │          │
           └──────────┘
           deconstruction  t
```

a. violates Condition C

b. violates Condition B (Chomsky 1986, p.8) an (R-expression is free B). A pronominal is free in its GC (A is the governing category for B if A is the minimal category contraining B and a governor of B, where A= NP or S (Chomsky 1981b, p.188)

4. Chomsky (1986b) does refer to genitive when dealing with the following NP:

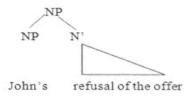

```
        NP
      /    \
   NP       N'
            /_____\
 John's    refusal of the offer
```

He assumes that if sisterhood is defined in terms of lexical projections, the subject will be indirectly θ-marked by the head of a nominal (or a gerundive) such as refusal (p.14).

5. Small Clause seems to be a constellation of phrase categories:

a. I thought [AP John unhappy]

b. I thought [NP John a great friend]

c. I expect [PP John in my office]

d. I saw [VP John leave]

6. No movement transformation can downgrade constituents because every moved constituent must c-command each one of its traces at s-structure (Haegeman 1991, p .481)

7. Stowell (1989, p. 240) noted that the possessor role may not be assigned to PRO

8. Benmamoun assumes that the CS (in Arabic) is basically a DP the governor of which is base generated

as complement of D, namley NP, and then gets moved
up to D as follows:

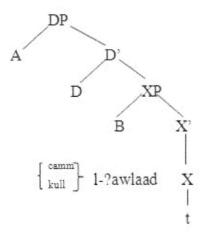

3. Logical Form

Broadly speaking, LF has to do with problems of meaning, ENTAILEMENT/ IMPLICATURES, WHOLE/PART, GF/ ROLES, DEEP/SURFACE STRUCTURES. It excludes however SOCIAL CONOTATIONS and HISTORICAL ETYMOLOGY.

Consider (1):

(1)

a. Tom stole two onions and a green pepper

b. It's cold in here

(1a) entails *Tom stole three things*, *Tom stole something* and *Tom did something* and *something happened*. (Smith & Wilson 1980), (1b) more than conveys a piece of information about the weather, it requires the hearer to be kind and considerate enough as to close the door.

Now, it would be nice to have a one-to-one correlation between form and meaning, some kind of Montague grammar based on Leibniz monadic whole/part view. Montague tried to relate syntactic categories and semantic concepts in a neat one-to-one correspondence (See Ben Rochd 1994a).

This is challenged however by idioms such as "kick the bucket" and non-concatenation. It is actually challenged by simple ordinary sentences, such as

(2)

a. John died

b. John is easy to please

c. John wants to please

Although John surfaces as the subject in sentence (2b) it is in fact the recipient of the action rather than the doer, likewise in (2a) John has done no action whatsoever; for obvious reasons.

There is no parallelism between PF, syntax, and LF. In Arabic, a nomination NP is end-marked /u/ and is agent, an objective NP is end-marked /a/ and functions as theme, an obligation NP is end-marked /i/ and is sometimes possessive or locative.

(3)

Daraba Zaidun   Bakran   fi   d-daari

Hit Zaid-NOUN   Bakr – OBJ   in def – house- OBL

         AGENT   THEME
LOCATIVE

3.1. Word Meaning

Some may think that the words of a language are totally independent. From the semantic point of view, however, the words are better seen as an intricate network of sense relations; such as ANTONYMY (day/night), HYPONOYMY (vehicle/ Rolls Royce), POLYSEMY (glasses) (See Ben Rochd 1994a).

3.1.1. HISTORICAL PERSPECTIVE

From the historical point of view, words are born, acquire successive layers of meaning and may eventually die. According to Grubb words such as cad were obsolete in 1980.

According to Bloomfield (1930) meaning can either go through a process of WIDENING or NARROWING. We could add SHIFTING. Consider (4)

a. doctor

b. ready

c. /muflis/

In the Old English *ready* meant "someone was ready to ride a horse", unlike in English where it generally means "be prepared for action or use" as in (5):

(5) The chicken are ready to eat

(6)

a. Comer (Spanish)

b. Chinois

c. saacah

In (6a) *comer* is a verb denoting "to eat". In Moroccan Arabic it shifted to a noun and was narrowed to "bread".

189

The word /saacah/, in Arabic, will mean "a gold watch" for a riche Arab oil prince nowadays. But in olden Arabia, it is used to mean "any lapse of time less than a day". So an hour (the 60 mn hour we know) would be /saacah/ just as 4, 6 or 8 hours. In the Holy Koran, it took a second meaning. It became "The Hour of Final Judgment". A third meaning was added then the "60 mn time" were discovered. And finally, a fourth meaning was associated with the word "saacah" which is the instruments for telling time "the watch/clock..". So /saacah/ now means all these (plus "now" as used in /hatta s-aacah/" ("up-to-now").

3.1.2. SOCIAL PERSPECTIVE[8]

Language is socially determined as far as connotative meaning is concerned. Bad words (such as "shut up") can either give a laugh to a friendly audience of the London café or be shocking to the *petit bourgeois* (or Yankee) although it was used from Chauser to Larkin- including Tenneson, who was a gentleman by any standards. (Grabb, p.c)

The word "guys" seems to refer to males only in England while in the US, a group of females is perfectly referred to as "guys". "qawm" ("people") unlike general belief, refers to men only as testified by the poetic verse

(7)   آل قصر ام نساء   و ما أدري أقوم

---

[8] Whatever is acceptable and valued in a given society will be devalued and rejected in another. "Bigamy" is devalued while "wine" is valued in the Western system. The other-way-round is prevalent in Islam.

I do not know whether men those of the castle or females.

3.1.3. DISTINCTIVE FEATURES[9]

From the logical perspective, each word has its own "personality" as it were, or what is known as DISTINCTIVE FEATURES and LOGICAL FORM. So a word such as *frighten* needs to be followed by an object that has the feature [+ animate]. Therefore (8b) is unacceptable:

(8)

a. Sincerity may frighten the boy

[+ animated]

b. * the boy may frighten sincerity

[+ abstracte]

[- animate]

The semantic[10] description can rely on distinctive features as in Semantic Cuisine. The following components are involved in the cooking vocabulary:

(9)

a. boil: [+ fire] [+ liquid]

b. fry: [+ fire] [+ fat]

---

[9] Chomsky (1967)
[10] Lethler

c. roast: [+ fire] [+ direct][11]

[+ fire] is not crucial while the second set of features do distinguish the cooking verbs *boil*, *fry* and *roast*.

3.1.4. MORPHOLOGICAL PERSPECTIVE

From the morphological perspective, Arabic seems to be a special case. Each word has a structure based on a three literal root such as k-t-b which conveys based on a hyponemic notion which is then refined into more specific notions by the insertion of vowels.

(10)

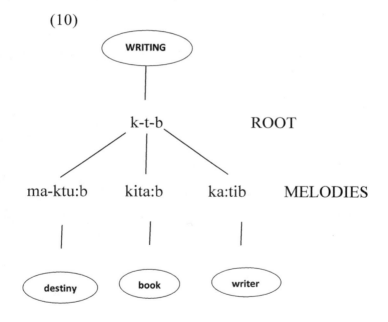

---

[11] Ben Rochd (1994a)

3.2. Sentence Meaning (LF)

3.2.1. Predicate Calculus

Truth is either INTENSIONAL or EXTENSIONAL[12] Logicians however are mainly concerned with the former. The truth value of each proposition is fixed by binary system (1/0). Truth is assigned 1 while falsehood is assigned 0.

Likewise in a SYLOGISM (consisting of three propositions, viz. MAJOR PREMISE, MINOR and CONCLUSION) the truth of the conclusion depends on the truth of the premises.

(11)

a. All men are morals

b. Socrates is a man

c. Socrates is mortal

1*1 Gives you **1, 0*1** Gives you **0, 0*1** Gives **0**

Propositions can be reanalyzed in predicate calculus as in (12):

(12)

a. narrow (table) ----> - large (table)   0

---

[12] ANALTIC PROPSITION is one whose grammatical form and lexical meaning it necessarily true, e.g. *spinsters are unmarried women.* By contrast a SYNTHETIC PROPSITION is one whose truth can be verified only by using empirical criteria, e.g. *those dogs are fierce.*

b. friend x, y (reversible)

c. think x, [P]

d. brother x, y (partially reversible)

f. father x, y (non-reversible)

g. out of   x, y

           [- abstract] [- abstract]

           [Part] [Whole]

i. in (static)

j. into (dynamic)

The term LOGICAL FORM has two meanings. One in the philosophical tradition going back to the greeks (and later developed by people like Wittgenstein and Russel) and the other in TG literature. The first one developed mainly in opposition to SUBSTANCE. A sentence like (12) may be either true or false depending on two factors, first: we ask do we have an entity called 'the king of France' and in case this entity exists, does it have the property of 'being bald'. Now, we know that France is a republic since 1987. So that entity does not exist. Therefore (13) is false. In TG, this term has a related, although somewhat different sense. In TG, theory suggests that the human mind/brain contains a component which assigns a structural description to each sentence. It is related to two other component PF (phonetic form) and LF (Logical form). The latter helps us assign the right interpretation to the sentence we come across. So in sentence (14) for instance, anyone who knows English knows that 'the idiot' can refer to 'John' but cannot refer to 'John's father', and this seems to be true in any other language that we know. This fact strongly supports the UG (universal grammar) hypothesis.

(13) The king of France is bald

(14) John's father knows that the idiot will never pass

(14) John's father knows that he will succeed

Chomsky defends that *"syntax deals with mental representations and their form, not with relations between language and the world. I know of very little work in linguistics (or any other field that deals with actual questions of reference, language use, etc., The reason is that studies of (true) semantics or pragmatics must be based on an account of the structure of language that is correct, not one that is wrong"*.

3.2.2. Binding Theory

In Chomsky (1992) Binding conditions are revisited as follows:

(15)

A) If A is an anaphora, interpret it as coreferential with a c-commanding phrase in D

B) If A is a pronominal, interpret it as disjoint from every c-commanding phrase in D

C) If A is an r-expression, interpret it as disjoint from every c-commanding phrase

(Where D is the relevant local domain)

This is illustrated in (16)

(16)

a. John saw himself

b. John saw him

c. John saw Fred

d. you said he liked [the pictures that John took]

e. [how many pictures that John took] did you say he liked t

f. Who [t said] he liked [how many pictures that John took]]

In (16d), *he c-commands John* and cannot take *John* as antecedent; in (16e), there is no c-command relation and *John* can be the antecedent of *he*. In (16f), *John* again cannot be the antecedent of he. Since the Binding properties of (c) are those of (a), not (b), we conclude that he c-commands John at the level of representation at which Conditions (C) applies.

(17) [[how many] who] [t said liked [[t' pictures] that John took]]

The answer, then, could be the pair (Bill, 7), meaning that "Bill said he liked 7 pictures that John took".

(18)

John wondered [which picture of himself] [Bill took it]

Consider (18). As before, himself can take either John or Bill as antecedent. There is a further ambiguity: the phrase take... pictures can be interpreted either IDIOMATICALLY (in the sense of "photograph") or LITERALLY ("pick up and walk away with"). (Chomsky 1992).

3.3. Idiomatics

Idioms have special structures. Consider (19):

(19)

a. You are the man in the house

b. You are out of my mind

c. To kick the bucket

"You are the man in the house" said by a father a father to his 4 years old kid was puzzling". He thought "I am not a man yet" and "in the house" sounded redundant to him. The idiomatic meaning of (19a) is "you are responsible after my departure, so watch!"

"You are out of your mind", "out of" is a complex preposition which denotes a movement of the part out of the whole both being [+ concrete] as in:

(20)

Get out of the garage

Now, "out of my mind" is a movement of the whole out of the part. The latter being abstract.

(21)

A: Have you ever kicked the bucket?

B: I can't have, I am writing a book

C: Well, Saussure did

3.4. Contradiction

According to Fromkin & Rodman (1983), a complete description of linguistic knowledge must involve a number of different types of rules.

A minority of sentences can be recognized as true by virtue of linguistic knowledge alone. Such sentences are called ANALYTIC.

(22)

a. Babies are not adults

b. Those dogs are fierce

The semantic component of a grammar should be able to state which sentences of the language were SYNONYMOUS, which were CONTRADICTORY or ANOMALOUS etc…

3.4.1. PREDICATIVES

The logical equivalent of a sentence is called a PROPOSITION. According to Al-Akhdari[13], there are 8 types of propositions:

(23)

a. Singular

b. Particular

c. Partially Quantified

d. Universally Quantified

(24)

a. Mr X is clever

b. Man is an island

c. Some people are poets

d. Every man is an island

---

[13] Al-Akhdari ; Arab logician of the 16th c.

Each of these can be either POSITIVE or NEGATIVE; which makes their number amount to eight.

3.4.2. CONDITIONALS

A conditional statement is based on ANTECEDENT and CONSEQUENT. The latter depends on the first. There are two types of conditionals: CATEGORIL/RIAL and DIJUNCTIVE.

1. BOUND: the second clause will fail if the first fails.

(25) If the sun rises it is day-time

There is a CAUSALITY link between the two clauses of Conditional type 1. This is a strict causality (analytic and synthetic).

3.4.3. DISJUNCTIVE

In disjunctive, the second clause can fail although the first occurs as in:

(26) If the day comes up the cocks will chant

Habitually, the cocks chant when the sun comes up but sometimes they do not. The probability is big but not absolute. Notice here a degradation in the scale of CERTAINTY from the strict/absolute link between CAUSE/EFFECT to habitual with exceptions to SPLIT:

(27)

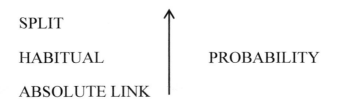

SPLIT

HABITUAL   PROBABILITY

ABSOLUTE LINK

CONDITIONAL TYPE 2 divides into 3 subclasses: no unity, no absence, neither nor

2.1. EXCLUSIVE (one of which is true)

(28) the car is either white or black

The car will be either "white" or "black". Two cases that cannot co-occur in reality, but can also be missing.

2.2. EXCLUSIVE (none can be true)

This is either non-white or non-black

They can co-occur in "red" for instance, but cannot be both missing (white & black).

2.3. NEITHER NOR

(29) The wall is either built or destroyed

The formulae for the above three cases in (30)

(30)

a. P   v   Q

b. not P   v   not Q

201

c. P   v not P

or table (34)

(31)	co-occur	co-miss
1	-	+
2	+	-
3	-	-

The last one is the most important and leads us to talk about contradiction.

According to Leech (1977), TAUTOLOGIES are vacuous informationally. At the opposite side of acceptability are CONTRADICTIONS, or statements which are, by virtue of meaning, necessarily false:

(32)

a. Life is life

b. Everything I like I dislike

CONTRADICTIONS are more decidedly deviant than TAUTOLOGIES: they are not just informationaly vacuous, but are drown right nonsensical:

(33)

a. is a contradiction

b. is invariably false

(34) This orphan has a father

[+ child]

[- mother]

[- father]   [+ father]

It might be predicted, for example that contradiction just would not occur in every day speech, performance factors are liable to interfere, for example, tautologies and contradictions actually do occur in conversation, but usually will some special interpretation involved such as irony, metaphor, and hyperbole[14]: *The child is father of the man, $_6$ I literally died of laughter when I saw him,* etc.

Some types of tautology and contradiction, too, can be defined in terms of hyponymy and as in

(35)

a. white is while (tautology)

b. This poorman has money (contradiction)

The rule of contradiction is the opposite of that for tautology: for one place predications, the rule is that the argument is incompatible with the predicate:

(36) The tennis I like is food

---

[14] Wordsworth

For two-place predications, the qualifying predication PN$_2$ is inconsistent with the remainder of the main predication:

(37)

People who like tennis hate games

Perhaps the most important type of contradiction is an assertion which is logically inconsistent with one of its presuppositions:

(38)

The illiterate soldier was reading a newspaper[15] presupposed and is inconsistent with:

Whenever (39a) is true, (39b) must be false and vice versa. They are thus, by our definition, contradictories. Similarly, a sentence may be said to be a contradiction because it has contradictory entailments. Thus (40) is a contradiction because it entails both (41) and (41)

(40) life is not life

(41) ? A sprister is not a woman

(41) is of course intuitively, a contradiction. The entailments we have in mind are (42a) and (42b)

(42) a. An unmarried woman is not a woman

---

[15] If you give a book to an illiterate soldier, he will take it up-side-down, and all he will see is barbed wire.

b. An unmarried woman is a woman

Contradictory sentences are always false.

Two sentences may be said to be contradictories if each entails the negation of the other. Thus (42a) and (42b) are contradictions:

(43)

a. No one has led a perfect life

b. Someone has led a perfect life

Whenever (42 a) is true (42b) must be false, and whenever (42b) is true, (42a) must be false. They are necessarily true and necessarily false.

Open and *closed* are said to be contradictory antonyms because from *The door is not open* we can infer *The door is closed*, and vice versa.

According to Crystal (1988), contradiction is a term sometimes used in SEMANTICS to refer to a SENSE relation between lexical items. Contradictory terms display a type of oppositeness of MEANING, illustrated by such pairs as *male/female* and *single/married*. Because of the technical use of this terms in logic (where it refers to a relationship between two propositions such that they cannot both be true and both be false).

Complex propositional formulae are true irrespective of what particular propositions are substituted for. The propositional (variables) are called tautology, and those that are false under the same conditions are contradictions. P&P is a tautology and P& -P is a contradiction.

3.4.4. Contradiction[16]

There are 10 CONDITIONS for a statement to be called a CONTRADICTION: it is the COMBINATION of two propositions that should share ten logical categories $_8$. One of the two propositions is NEGATIVE while the other is POSITIVE:

(44)   **P**   **&**   **not P**

[α CONDITION]   [CONDITIONα]

[α SUBJECT]   [α SUBJECT]

[α PREDICATE]   [α PREDICATE]

[α TIME]   [α TIME]

[α PLACE]   [α PLACE]

[α WHOLE]   [α WHOLE]

[α PART]   [α PART]

[α POTENTIAL]   [α POTENTIAL]

[α FACTUAL]   [α FACTUAL]

---

[16] Bouabid (p.c)

[α MODIFICATION]   [α MODIFICATION]

(45) John is clever and stupid

(45) is a contradiction. It consists of two propositions which share the same (implicit) ten logical categories (or entailments, mentioned above). Consider now (46):

(46)

a. John is generous and Paul is not

b. It rains in Alaska and it does not in Rabat (day/ night)

c. It was raining yesterday and it is not raining today

d. This student will succeed if he works hard and he will not succeed if he does not work hard

e. 2 is half 4 and not half 10

The above sentences are not contradictions as they do not share the above mentioned logical categories.

Appendix : TRANSFORMATIONS

    T.G. Standard Theory appeared in Chomsky's Aspect of the Theory of Syntax (1965). This theory consists of the following rules: phrase structure rules, lexical rules and transformational rules. Transformational rules apply on full structures to yield new sentences/structures. They are the link between two semantically related structures called Deep structure and Surface structure. We can say that transformational rules preserve the basic meaning of sentences but change their form. Some of the attested transformations assumed in the standard theory are, passive, raising, dative, relativization, etc... They are respectively exemplified as follows:

(1)

a. PASSIVE

the boy hit the ball ---------> the ball was hit by the ball

b. RAISING

it is easy to please John ---------> John is easy to please

c. DATIVE

I gave a book to Mary ---------> I gave Mary a book

d. RELATIVIZATION

the cat chased the rat ---------> the cat that chased the rat

e. CAUSATIVE

je fais le cheval boit l'eau ---------> je fais boire le cheval

f. REFLEXIVIZATION

John saw John ---------> John saw himself

g. NORMINILIZATION

the enemy destroyed the city ---------> the destruction of the city

h. IMPRATIVE

you help yourself ---------> help yourself

i. TOPCALIZATION

we trust in God ---------> in God, we trust

j. PIED-PIPING

you are talking about what ---------> what are you talking about

k. EXTRAPOSITION

a protest about wages has started ---------> a protest has started about wages

a. PASSIVE

NP1+ V+ NP2 ---------> NP2+ V+ by NP1

b. RAISING

V+ Adj.P + V+ NP ---------> NP+ V+ Adj.P + VP

c. DATIVE

NP1+ V+ NP 2 + to NP3 ---------> NP1+ V+ NP3+ NP2

d. RELATIVZATION

NP 1+ VP ---------> NP 1+ who/that+ VP

e. CAUSATIVE

NP1+ V1+ NP2+ V2+ NP3 ---------> NP1+ V1+ V2+ NP2

f. REFLEXIVIZATION

NP1+ V+ NP2 ---------> NP1+ V+ REF. PRO

g. NOMINALIZATION

NP+ V+ NP ---------> NP PP

h. IMPERATIVE

NP1+ V+ NP 2 ---------> V+ NP 2

i. TOPICALIZATION

NP+ V+ PP ---------> PP+ NP V

j. EXTRAPOSITION

NP+ VP ---------> NP+ VP+ PP

k. PIPPING

$$\text{NP1}+ \text{V}+ \text{NP2}+ \text{PP} \text{ ---------}> \begin{Bmatrix} \text{PP} \\ \text{NP} \end{Bmatrix} + \text{be}+ \text{NP 1}+ \text{V}$$

$$+ \text{NP 2} \begin{Bmatrix} \varnothing \\ \text{P} \end{Bmatrix}$$

PIED PIPING

(3) What are you looking at that woman like that for?

In the legend for Hamlin it is said that a city was invaded, by mice, and later saved by a piper who was playing a flute. Once the mice heard his music, they came out of the city following the man and were drowned into the sea. *The city and the mice* are the PP, while the NP is the mice alone.

(4)

you are talking [about [what]] ?

what are you talking about?

What about are you talking?

Both questions are surface structures of:

you are talking about what

RELATIVIZATION involves an NP-movement and the adjunction of a relative pronoun as in:

(5)

d-s: <u>the dog</u>   <u>chased the rat</u>

    X   Y

    X   wh-/that   Y

s-s : <u>the dog</u> that <u>chased the rat</u>

According to Suaieh (1980), in Arabic the relative pronoun appears between a clitic pronoun to its right and a noun phrase to its left. The three items are semantically coreferential and hence coindexed. Syntactically, they must agree in number, gender and person, as follows:

(6)

a. NP_i RP_i CL_i

b.   <u>?al-mar?atyu</u>   l<u>lati:</u>   ra ?ajtu-<u>ha</u>

The same agreement relations should hold at surface and deep structures. Consider (7)

(7)

one of the students that strike (s) my attention as intelligent.

(8)

213

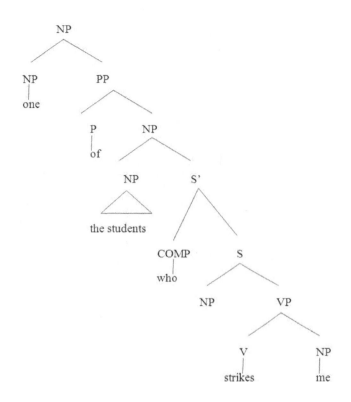

s-s: one of the students who strikes me as intelligent.

d-s: one of the students strikes me as intelligent.

Restrictive relative clauses are adjuncts whereas non-restrictive relative clauses are complements (Radford 1988). Consider the following noun phrase:

(10)

His wife who lives in Dublin/Rabat

(10) is ambiguous as in polygamous community, she would be the second or third wife whereas in a

monogamous society, the relative clause is merely descriptive (vs restrictive). Syntactically, the first reading is rendered by adjunction whereas the second is rendered by complementation.

DESCRIPTIVE

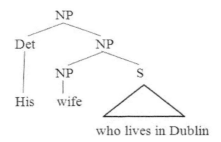

who lives in Dublin

RESTRICTIVE

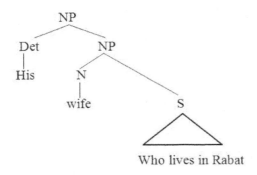

Who lives in Rabat

X-bar notations (viz., Adjuncts vs complementation) may explain ambiguity still better:

DESCRIPTIVE

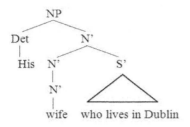

RESTRICTIVE

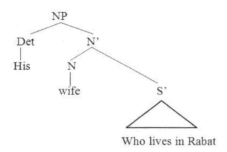

The same is applicable to (13)

(13) The boy saw the man with the telescope

This sentence means either that *the boy* used *the telescope* to see *the man*, or that *the boy* saw *the man* who happened to have *a telescope*.

TRANSFORMATIONS are also needed to clear away the discrepancy between SUBJECT and DOER OF THE ACTION as in

(14)

a. John passed away

b. John killed the albatross

In (14a) *John* is the subject but by no means the doer of the action (for obvious reasons!). In (14b) *John* is the subject and also the doer of the action. To quote Rodman and Fromkin (1983), we must distinguish the LOGICAL SUBJECT in (b) from the STRUCTURAL SUBJECT in (a), i.e., the first NP of the highest clause.

Another example is found in raising:

(15)

John is easy to please

EXTRAPOSITION

The obligatory presence of certain constituency in a sentence can be accounted for in terms of lexical entry.

(16)

a. he amazed me

b. * John amazed

c. * amazed me

d. * John amazed me it

e. That John likes bananas amazed me

f. It amazed me that John likes bananas

g. amaze : V [{ NP/S'} _ NP]

The extraposed constituent is not a referring expression. It does not refer to an ENTITY IN THE WORLD, a person, an object. It cannot be questioned. It plays no role in the SEMANTIC MAKE UP of the sentence. Its presence is for mere STRUCTURAL REASONS. This is the case of the extraposed PP of *my book*.

(17)

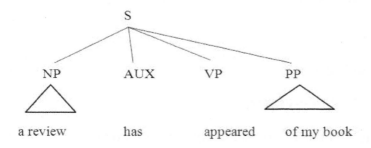

There is a PP constituent in PS rules. But it is different from the extraposed PP.

(18)

S ⟶ NP Aux VP PP

VP ⟶ V

NP ⟶ Det N

PP ⟶ P NP

V ⟶ appear

Aux ⟶ has

P $\longrightarrow$ of

N $\longrightarrow$ review, book

Det $\longrightarrow$ a, by

PP $\longrightarrow$ at noon   in Paris   for a good reason

                 TIME   PLACE   REASON

Extraposed constituents cannot be inserted into unfilled PP –positions. There is no sentence – final position, so the moved item must go to a POSITION CREATED FOR IT.

The conflict PS rules   NP   VP   (PP)   vs Extraposition is solved by the following configuration:

(19)[$_{NP}$ It [$_{VP}$ apperead [$_{PP}$ at noon]]

                      [in Paris]

                      [for a good reason]

                      [of my book]

(20)

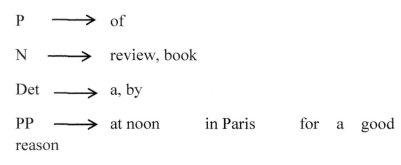

                         of my book

a review   appeared

Some sentences need more than one transformation and/or the application of a transformation more than once in a certain order known as the **CYCLE**. Consider (21).

(21) the bomb was believed to have been planted by the IRA.

The deep structure of (21) would be as follows:

(22) [$_{S1}$ the authorities believed [$_{S2}$ the IRA planted the bomb]]

First, PASSIVE must apply to S_2 which yields:

(23) [$_{S1}$ the authorities believed [$_{S2}$ the bomb be planted by the IRA]]

Then SUBJECT-TO-OBJECT RAISING would move *the bomb* to make it the object of S_1 as in (24):

(24) [$_{S1}$ the authorities believed the bomb [$_{S1}$ be planted by the IRA]]

Finally PASSIVE applies to the object of S1 the bomb, moving it to the subject position, yielding (25):

(25) the bomb was believed to have been planted by the IRA.

The cycle forces the transformations to apply in a certain order from the lowest sentence to the top one, in our case: passive, raising and passive. One of the most important traditional arguments for the cycle is based on sentence like (25).

(26)

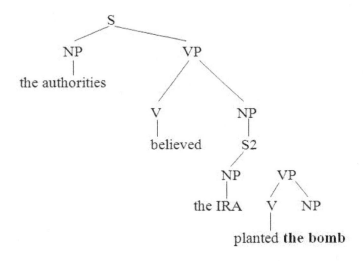

(27)

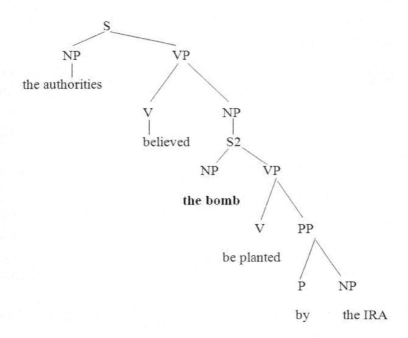

In the derivation of (25) from (22), passive applies to S_2, producing the derived structure. Subject-to-Object Raising then raises the bomb, making it the derived object of S_1. This produces the structure:

(28)

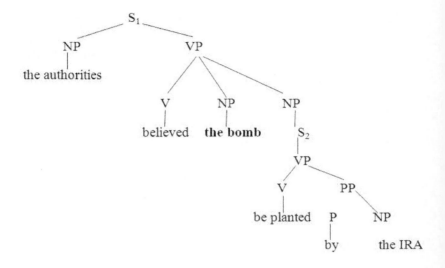

Finally, Passive applies in S_1 resulting in

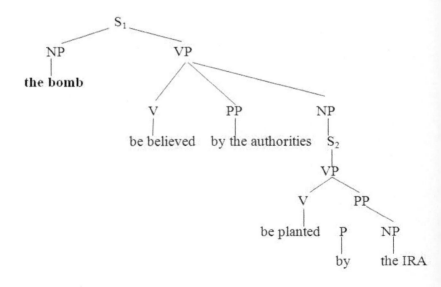

(29)

Notice how *the bomb* moved from bottom to top.

Another example of the cycle is to be found in the following sentence:

(30)

I am a man sinned against

The deep structure of which would be (31):

(31)

_ be a man [someone sinned against me]

Passive then raising would apply to it as in (32) and (33):

(32)

_ be a man [I sinned against me]

 (33)

I am a man [sinned against]

I am a man more sinned against than sinning

(Shakespear)

REFERENCES

Abdel Ghany, M. (1981) *Government-Binding in Classical Arabic*. Ph.D. Austin. Texas University.

Abdu-Ghany, A. (1981) <u>Government-Binding in Classical Arabic</u>, Ph.D, University of Texas at Austin.

Abney, S. (1986) "Functional Elements and Licensing", ms, MIT, Cambridge, Mass.

Allen J & P. Van Buren. (1957) *Chomsky: Selected Readings,* OUP, Oxford.

Allwood J., Anderson L. & O. Dahl. (1987) *Logic in Linguistics*, CUP, Cambridge

Akmajian, A. & F. Heny. (1975) *Introduction to the Principles of Transformational Syntax*, MIT, Cambridge, Mass.

Al Seghayar, M. (1988) *On the Syntax of Small Clauses in Arabic*, MA, Ottawa University.

Al-Shorafat, M. (1991) "Case Assignment in Arabic and the GB Theory," *Linguistica Communicatio* 3-2.

Al Waer, M. (1981) "An Interview with Noam Chomsky", ms, MIT.

Allwood, J. Andersson, L. & O. Dahl. (1987) *Logic in Linguistics*, CUP, Cambridge.

Ancton, O. (1994) "Notes on the Optionality of AGR," ms, University of Washington.

Aoun, J. (1985) *A Grammar of Anaphora*, MIT, Cambridge, Mass.

Aoun, J. (1986) Generalized Binding. Doedrecht: Foris

Barwise J & J. Etchemendy. (1993) Tarski's World, CSLI, Stanford.

Benmamoun, E. (1993) "Null Pronominal in the Context of NP and QP," ms, US California.

Ben Rochd, E. (1982) *French Passive*, MA., York University.

Ben Rochd, E. (1990) *Pronominilization*, Ph.D UC University.

Ben Rochd, E. (1991a) "Arabic & Barriers", *Linguistica Communicatio*.

Ben Rochd, E. (1991b) "J. Aoun's Generalized Binding & Arabic Evidence", *Revue de la Facultés des Lettres*, Oujda.

Ben Rochd, E. (1991c) 'Barriers and Arabic'. *Linguistica Communicatio III*.

Ben Rochd, E. & M. Khris (1993) *Schools of Linguistics*, Takafia, Casabalanca. (ARABIC)

Ben Rochd, E. (1994a) *Generative Grammar*, Takafia, Oujda.

Ben Rochd, E. (1994b) *Linguistic Theory in America*, Jadida, Casablanca. (ARABIC)

Ben Rochd, E. (1995) *Arabic and Semantics*. Ms. University of Washington.

Ben Rochd, E. (1995b) *Form & Meaning –Face to Face: Non-Concatenation, Logical Form & Idiomatics*. University of British Columbia. Canada.

Ben Rochd, E. (1997a) 'X-bar, DP, Occam's Razor and LF in Arabic'. *Bulletin of the Faculty of Humanities and Social Sciences*. Vol. 20, University of Qatar.

Ben Rochd, E. (1997b) *The Evolution of Transformational Grammar*. Oujda, Oriental.

Ben Rochd, E. (1999a) *Arabic & Logical Form*. Casablanca, Dechra.

Ben Rochd, E. (1999b) "Arabic, Origins, Structure and Most Outstanding Grammarian: Sibawaihi". *Revue de la Faculte des Letteres* . Numero 7. Oujda.

Ben Rochd, E. (2001) "Sibawaihi, The Syntactician". *Revue de la Faculte des Letteres* . Numero 4. Beni Mellal.

Ben Rochd, E. (2019) *Traditions in linguistics*. Books-on-Demand

Ben Rochd, E. (2019) *Sibawaihi's Transformational Grammar*. Books-on-Demand

Ben Rochd, E. (2020) *Generative Grammar*. Books-on-Demand

Beneveniste, E. (1966) *Problème de la linguistique générale*, Galimard, Paris.

Bittner, M & K. Hale. (1993) 'Ergavity', ms, MIT.

Bloomfield, L. (1993) *Language*, Holt, New York.

Borer, H. (1983) <u>*Parametric Syntax*</u>, Foris, Dordrecht.

Borer, H. (1989) "Anaphoric AGR", Jaegli.

Bresnan, J. (1970a) "An Argument against Pronominalization," <u>*Linguistics Inquiry*</u> 1, 122-23.

Brusse, W. (1974) *Klasse Transitivitat Valenz*, Fink, Munich.

Carter, M. (1968) *A Study of Sibawaihi's Principles of Grammatical Analysis*, Ph.D, Oxford University.

Chomsky, N. (1957) *Syntactic Structures*, Mouton, The Hague.

Chomsky, N. (1965) *Aspects of the Theory of Syntax*, MIT, Cambridge.

Chomsky, N. (1972) *Language & Mind*, Harcourt Brace & Joeavich.

Chomsky, N. (1972) *Studies on Semantics in Generative Grammar*. The Hague. Mouton.

Chomsky, N. (1977) "On Wh-Movement," <u>*Formal Syntax*</u>, Academic Press, New York.

Chomsky, N. (1981) *Lectures on Government & Binding*, Foris, Dordrecht.

Chomsky, N. (1982) *Some Concepts & Consequences of the Theory of GB*, MIT, Cambridge, Mass.

Chomsky, N. (1986b) *Barriers*, MIT, Cambridge, Mass.

Chomsky, N. (1988) *Language & Problems of Knowledge*, MIT, Cambridge, Mass.

Chomsky, N. & H. Lasnik. (1991) "Principles & Parameters Theory", ms, MIT, Cambridge, Mass.

Chomsky, N. (1992) "A Minimalist Program for Linguistic Theory", ms, MIT, Cambridge, Mass.

Chomsky, N. (1994) "Bare Phrase Structures", ms, MIT, Cambridge, Mass.

Chomsky, N. (1995) *The Minimalist Program*. Cambridge. MIT.

Comrie, B. (1989) *Language Universals & Linguistic Typology*, Blackwell, Oxford.

Comrie, B. (1990) 'On the Importance of Arabic for General Linguistic Theory'. *Perspectives on Arabic Linguistics*. University of Southern California.

Crystal, D. (1985). *A Dictionary of Linguistics & Phonetics*. Oxford: Basil Blackwell.

Emonds, J. (1976). *A Transformational Approach to English Syntax*, AP, NY.

Emonds, J. (1987). "Parts of Speech in Generative Grammar," *Linguistic Analysis* 17, 1-42.

Evans, T. (1972) "Chomsky", *Brain Research Association*, London.

Fassi-Fihri, A. (1989) "Agreement, Incorporation, Pleonastics, " ms, MIT, Cambridge, Mass.

Fiengo, R. (1977) "Trace Theory," *Linguistic Inquiry* 8, 35-61.

Fromkin, V. & R. Roman (1983) *An Introduction to Language*, Holt-Saunders, New York.

Gazar, G. (1979) "Unbounded Dependencies & Coordinate Structures," *Linguistic Inquiry,* 12, 155-184.

Gleason, H. (1969) *An Introduction to Descriptive Linguistics*, Hold, New York.

Guéron, J. (1984) "Extraposition & Logical Form", *Linguistic Inquiry*, 15, 1-30.

Guéron, J. & R. May (1988) "Les chaînes: T et les verbes auxiliéres", *Lexique*, Université de Lille III.

Haegem, L. (1991) *An Introduction to Government & Binding Theory*, Blackwell, Oxford.

Halle, K. (1983) "Warlpiri & the Grammar of Non-configurational Languages", *Natural Language & Linguistic Theory*, 1, 5-47.

Hoeksema, J. (1987) "Logic of Natural Language", *Linguistic Analysis*, 11n 155-184.

Huddleston, R. (1976) *An Introduction to English Transformational Syntax*, Longman, London.

Jackendoff, R. (1977) *X-bar Sytax: A Study of Phrase Structure*, MIT, Cambridge, Mass.

Ibn Jinni (1952) Al-Khasa'is. Cairo

Kayne, R. (1975) *French Syntax: the Transformational Cycle*. Cambridge. MIT.

Kayne, R. (1987) "Null Subjects & Clitic Climbing," paper presented to GLOW, Venice.

Kayne, R. (1991) "Romance Clitics, Verb Movement, and PRO," *Linguistic Inquiry* 4, 647-686.

Khalaily, S. (1997) *One Syntax for All Categories*. The Hague H.I.L.

Kremers, JM. (2003) *The Arabic noun phrase a minimalist approach*. Katholieke UNiversiteit

Langacker, R. (1969) "On Pronominalization & the Chain of Command" *Modern Studies in English*. Ney Jersy: Prentice Hall.

Langacker, R. (1995) 'Cognitive Grammar' in *Concise History of the Language Sciences from the Sumerians to the Cognitivists*. Cambridge. Pergamon.

Lasnik, H. (1976) "Remarks on Conference". *Linguistic Analysis* 2, 1-22.

Lyle, J. (1995) "Adjunction of Antecedent Contained Deletion", NWLC, University of Victoria.

Lyons, J. (1975) *New Horizons in Linguistics*, Penguin, Middlesex.

Lyons, J. (1997) *Semantics*, CUP, Cambridge.

Madkour, I. (1969) *L'Organon dans le monde Arabe*, J. Vrin, Paris.

May, R. (1985) *Logical Form*, MIT, Cambridge, Mass.

McCarthy, J. (1979) *Formal Problems in Semitic Phonology & Morphology*, Ph.D., MIT, Cambridge, Mass.

Miller, D. (1983) *Popper*, Fontana, Oxford.

Miller, J. (1990) "Born Talking," BBC.

Newmeyer, J.F. (1980) *Linguistic Theory in America*, AP, New York.

Newmeyer, J.F. (1988) *The Cambridge Survey of Linguistics*, CUP, Cambridge.

Ouhalla, J. (1988) *The Syntax of Head Movement: A Berber Study*, Ph.D, UC London.

Ouhalla, J. (1989) "Clitic Movement & the ECP", *Lingua* 79, 165-215.

Ouhalla, J. (1994) "Verb Movement and Word Order in Arabic." *Lightfoot & Hornstein. CUP.*

Ouhalla, J. (2002) "The Structure and Logical Form of Negative Sentences in Arabic". *Themes in Arabic and Hebrew Syntax*, (ed. Jamal Ouhalla & Ur Shlonsky, Kluwer, Dordrecht.

Ouhalla, J. (2004) "Semitic Relatives." *Linguistic Inquiry*, Vol. 35, N 2, 288-300. M.I.T.

Palmer, F. (1983) *Grammar*, Penguin, Middlesex.

Palmer, F. (1990) *Semantics*, CUP, Cambridge.

Partee, B. (1975) "Montague Grammar & TG", *Linguistic Inquiry* 6, 203-300.

Pike, K. (1982) *Linguistic Concepts: An Introduction to Tagmentics*, University of Nebraska, Lincon.

Quirk, R. & S. Greenbaum. (1980) *A University Grammar of English*, Longman, London.

Radford, A. (1981) *Transformational Syntax*, CUP, Cambridge.

Radford, A. (1988) *Transformational Grammar*, CUP, Cambridge.

Riemsdjik, H & E. Williams. (1986) *Introduction to the Theory of Grammar*, MIT, Cambridge, Mass.

Rizzi, L. (1982) *Issues in Italian Syntax*, Foris, Dordrecht.

Ross, J. (1968) *Constraints on Variables in Syntax*, Ph.D., MIT, Cambridge, Mass.

Sampson, G. (1980) *Schools of Linguistics*, Hutchinson, London.

Saussure, F. (1977) *Course in General Linguistics*, Fontana, Oxford.

Sells, P. (1985) *Lectures on Contemporary Syntactic Theories*, CSLI, Sanford.

Sells, P. (1987) "Binding Presumptive Pronouns," *Linguistics & Philosophy* 10, 261-298.

Smith, N. & D. Wilson. (1979) *Modern Linguistics: The Results of Chomsky's Revolution*, Penguin, Middlesex.

Soams S. & D. Permutter. (1979) *Syntactic Argumentation & the Structure of English*, UCP, Los Angeles.

Souaieh, I. (1980) *Aspects of Arabic Relative Clauses*, Ph.D, Indiana University.

Souali, E. (1990) "DP, derived Nominals & Case Marking in Arabi," *Linguistica Communication*.

Stowell, T. (1989) 'Subjects, Specifiers & X-bar Theory', in M.R. Baltin & A.S. Kroach, eds. *Alternative conceptions of Phrase Structure*, University of Chicago Press, Chicago.

Tizaoui, H. (1995) *The Evolution of Chomsky's Syntactic Theory*, unpublished.

Tritton, S. (1943) *Arabic*, Teach yourself Books, Hodder & Stoughton.

Wasow, T. (1975) "Anaphoric Pronouns & Bound Variables", <u>Language</u> 51, 386- 373.

Wittgenstein, L. (1958) *Philosophical Investigations*, Blackwell, Oxford.

Wright, W. (1979) *A Grammar of the Arabic Language,* CUP, Cambridge.